The Economics of
Ludwig von Mises

The Economics of
Ludwig von Mises

Toward a Critical Reappraisal

Edited with an Introduction by
Laurence S. Moss

SHEED AND WARD, INC.
Subsidiary of Universal Press Syndicate
Kansas City

The Economics of Ludwig von Mises
Copyright © 1976 by the Institute for Humane Studies
All rights reserved. Printed in the United States of
America. No part of this book may be used or repro-
duced in any manner whatsoever without written per-
mission except in the case of reprints in the context of
reviews. For information write Sheed and Ward, Inc.,
6700 Squibb Road, Mission, Kansas 66202

Library of Congress Cataloging in Publication Data

Symposium on the Economics of Ludwig von Mises,   H B
Atlanta, 1974.   1 0 1
The economics of Ludwig von Mises.
                                                      V 66
                                                      59
(Studies in economic theory)
Includes bibliographical references and index.   1974
Appendices (p.   ): A. Chronology.—B.
Major translated writings of Ludwig von Mises.
   1. Von Mises, Ludwig, 1881-1973—Congresses.
I. Moss, Laurence S., 1944-   II. Title.
III. Series.
HB101.M6S9   1974   330.1   75-41380
ISBN 0-8362-0650-9
ISBN 0-8362-0651-7 pbk.

CONTENTS

PREFACE

In March 1974 I got in touch with Professor Leland Yeager, who was then president-elect of the Southern Economics Association, and told him that I wanted to organize a symposium on the economic thought of Ludwig von Mises for the November 1974 meeting of our association in Atlanta, Georgia. Mises had died in October 1973, and we would be meeting on nearly the first anniversary of his death. Yeager agreed that, although Mises had been named a "Distinguished Fellow" of the American Economics Association in September 1969, many economists were not well acquainted with either the content of his thought or the enormous range of subjects to which he had devoted more than seventy years of active scholarship. At a time when the cherished "idols" of the intellectual marketplace were being regarded with suspicion, and economists were becoming critical of their basic assumptions and methods, it seemed appropriate to devote an entire session to someone whose lifework had been on the foundations of the science. Thus, we had every reason to believe that a panel on Mises would be well attended and set to work deciding whom to invite and what aspects of Mises' contribution could be most profitably discussed in the short space of two hours.

Professors Murray N. Rothbard and Israel M. Kirzner were approached first: both were well-known students of Mises and had themselves extended Mises' contribution in several directions. Rothbard chose to reevaluate the famous debate on economic calculation in order to show that Mises' objections to centralized planning were more firmly grounded than his opponents imagined. Kirzner proposed to outline Mises' approach to capital and interest by contrasting it with the approaches of Eugen von Böhm-Bawerk, Frank H. Knight, and John Bates Clark.

A large portion of Mises' writing is concerned with the broad issues of political economy and sociology. On Rothbard's recommendation, we contacted Professor William Baumgarth, who agreed to prepare a paper on Mises' political philosophy, inasmuch as Baumgarth's own doctoral research on Friedrich Hayek's political thought had brought him into contact with Mises' writings. Finally, I chose to speak about Mises' contribution to monetary economics by emphasizing the use Mises made of the cash-balance mechanism in his treatment of monetary disturbances.

What our session lacked, by mid-April, was a chairman and principal discussant. Yeager wrote to Professor Fritz Machlup, whose friendship with Mises dated from the interwar period, when as a graduate student at the University of Vienna, he had participated in Mises' famous seminars in economic theory. Machlup agreed to chair the session, introduce its subject as well as the speakers, and close with evaluative critical comments on the papers presented. Finally, Professor Karen I. Vaughn consented to act as the principal discussant; it was her job to pull the session together by uncovering common themes in the four principal papers and offering criticism of what had been said. In this task she was joined by Machlup, whose penetrating final comments suggested further lines of research and contributed to the overall goal of our meeting, which was to promote interest in Mises' scientific contributions.

On Friday morning, 15 November 1974, our panel convened before an audience of nearly 200 economists. At the conclusion of the session nearly half that number responded to Professor Machlup's invitation to continue our discussions on an informal basis over a generous buffet luncheon hosted by the Institute for Humane Studies in the elegant Atlantis room of the Hyatt Regency Hotel, where the convention was being held. Thanks to the efforts of the panel participants, Professor Yeager, the other officers of the Southern Economics Association, and the Institute for Humane Studies, the meeting proved to be a great success. Many of us came away with the feeling that a beginning had been made in a scholarly reevaluation of Mises' thought, and, regardless of the outcome, our own understanding of the foundations of the science would be greatly improved as a by-product of this endeavor.

This book contains edited versions of the four principal papers presented at the conference and the edited transcripts of Machlup's and Vaughn's remarks and criticisms. In addition I have included two brief appendixes, one listing important dates in the life of Ludwig von Mises and the other listing Mises' most important translated writings.

I would like to thank George Pearson and Kenneth Templeton of the Institute for Humane Studies for their sincere interest in the work of the Austrian school of economics and, in particular, in the writings of Ludwig von Mises. Their encouragement in the form of expert advise and financial assistance was as essential to this enterprise as the work of the authors themselves. I would also like to thank each of the contributors to this volume, who have attended to deadlines and worked hard on the final stages of production. Fritz Machlup and Ilse Mintz furnished some of the biographical material I have included in the introduction. Finally I wish to thank my typist, Ms. Cynthia Annunziata, for her careful and thoughtful handling of the manuscript.

LAURENCE S. MOSS
University of Virginia
Charlottesville, Virginia

March 1975

Introduction

Laurence S. Moss

I

Ludwig von Mises was born on 29 September 1881 in the city of Lemberg of the Austro-Hungarian Empire (now city of Lvov, USSR). His father, Arthur Edler von Mises, was a construction engineer employed by the Austrian railroads, and his mother was the former Adele Landau.[1] Ludwig grew up and was educated in Vienna and in 1900 entered the University of Vienna, where he received the degree of doctor of jurisprudence in 1906. At the University he studied with Friedrich von Wieser and Eugen von Böhm-Bawerk, the followers of Carl Menger, the founder of the Austrian school of economics.[2]

In 1902, shortly after the publication of his first book (a historical study of the Galician peasants),[3] he was called to active duty in the Austro-Hungarian army. This service lasted only one year, and he was not called again to active duty until World War I (1914), when he served as captain of the artillery in the Russian Ukraine. Besides his military duty, Mises' public service included a position as chief of the finance department of the Austrian Chamber of Commerce, which appraised legislative proposals in the area of monetary and financial policy. Mises held this post from 1909 until 1934, when he left Austria to take a teaching position in Geneva, well in advance of the German invasion of Austria (March 1938).

In 1913, shortly after the publication of his remarkable and erudite *Theory of Money and Credit* (1912), Mises was named "professor extraordinary" at the University of Vienna. Although this professorial position did not carry a salary, it signaled Mises' emergence as one of the brilliant younger members of the Austrian

1

school of economics.[4] During the 1920s Mises won international recognition for his article on "economic calculation," which challenged the Socialist writers to explain how a meaningful set of relative price relationships could be established once socialism had abolished all markets for capital goods.[5]

In 1926 Mises toured the United States under the sponsorship of the Laura Spelman Rockefeller Memorial. When he returned to Austria in 1926, he established the Austrian Institute for Business Cycle Research. At that time Mises reformulated and expanded his monetary theory of the business cycle, first sketched in his 1912 study on money and credit mentioned previously. Many of Mises' articles and books containing elaborations and applications of his cycle analysis are still untranslated.[6] One route by which Mises' basic ideas did, however, reach a wider audience was through the lectures of his student Friedrich Hayek at the London School of Economics during the thirties.[7]

In addition to his work on business-cycle analysis and economic theory in general, Mises published on subjects as seemingly diverse as political liberalism and the philosophy of science. As a champion of economic liberalism he explained how an unhampered market economy acted as the best guarantee of peace and prosperity. On the special problems of the logic and structure of economic explanations, Mises argued the case for "methodological individualism," thereby furthering the valuable work already done by Carl Menger and Max Weber.[8] Two of Mises' important works, dating from this period, are translated under the titles *The Free and Prosperous Commonwealth* and *Epistemological Problems of Economics*[9].

In 1934 Mises accepted the offer of a professorship at the Graduate Institute of International Studies in Geneva, Switzerland.[10] In 1938, at the age of 57, he married Margit Sereny-Herzfeld.

In 1940 Mises immigrated to the United States. From 1940 to 1944 he was a guest of the National Bureau of Economic Research in New York and financed his writings by way of this and other research grants. With the exception of a visiting professorship for one year at the National University in Mexico, Mises did not return to teaching until 1945, when he was appointed visiting professor of the Graduate School of Business Administration at New York University. His publications during this period ranged from a systematic analysis of the deficiencies of bureaucracy to a final version of his masterwork on economics, *Human Action* (1949). The latter work synthesized his entire contribution to economics and placed the discipline of economics within the framework of an all-encompassing science of human action, which he termed "praxeology".

During the 1950s and 1960s Mises was honored on numerous occasions both in Europe and in the United States. His New York seminar was attended by prominent people from all walks of life, many of whom went on to become academic economists themselves.[11] Throughout this period Mises continued to contribute to the areas of philosophy of science, political philosophy, sociology, history, and economics. By 1969, when he retired from teaching, he had established himself as one of the most prolific scholars of the twentieth century. In 1969, shortly before his university retirement, Mises was named a "Distinguished Fellow" of the American Economics Association. The citation accompanying the award reads as follows:

A library possessing all the books by Ludwig von Mises would have nineteen volumes if it confined itself to first editions, forty-six volumes if it included all revised editions and foreign translations, and still more if it possessed the *Festschriften* and other volumes containing contributions by him. The stream of publications began in 1902. Mises will be 88 years old this September. He taught at the University of Vienna until 1934 and at the Institut Universitaire in Geneva until 1940. He still teaches at New York University. The stream of students that has come out of his seminars is no less remarkable than his literary output.

His published work ranges from economic history and history of thought to methodology and political philosophy, with special emphasis on monetary theory, international finance, business fluctuations, price and wage theory, industrial organization, and economic systems. It would not be possible to enumerate the ideas which Mises has originated and disseminated over the years, but some of the most fruitful may be mentioned: in monetary theory, the application of marginal utility theory to the explanation of the demand for money; in business cycle theory, certain amendments to the Wicksellian theory of the cumulative process and a demonstration that a monetary policy stabilizing certain price indices would not at the same time stabilize business activity; in the theory of socialist economic planning, the discovery that the type of economic calculation required for an efficient allocation of resources cannot be carried out without a system of competitive market prices. The recent movements toward decentralized planning in several Soviet-type economies add the endorsement of history to the insights at which Mises arrived almost fifty years ago.[12]

Mises' last public address was given in New York City on 2 May 1970, on the topic to which he devoted more than fifty years of thought, "Socialism versus the Free Market." He died on 10 October 1973 at the age 92. He was survived by his wife, Margit, his two stepchildren, Gitta Sereny Honeyman and Guido Sereny, his close personal friends and confidants Henry Hazlitt and Lawrence Fertig, and a host of students and admirers the world over. His personal library of 6,000 volumes is housed at Hillsdale College in Michigan.

II

How do we measure the extent of Mises' influence? By the test of avowed discipleship, there are few professional economists who call themselves "pure Misesians"; yet Mises had, as we have seen, a profound influence on many contemporary economists. Part of Mises' influence had to do with his seminar teaching: there was something unique and unforgettable about his manner and approach. As one who was fortunate enough to attend Mises' seminars in New York City (1963-65), I would like to recount some aspects of that experience.

Certainly, as a teacher of economics is expected to do, Mises communicated ideas, distinct policy proposals, and characteristic attitudes to his students. But above all he offered his students a reasonably consistent world outlook at a time when the economics profession was becoming increasingly fragmented and overly specialized. He presented a cogent and carefully thought out defense of the market and economic freedom that was as exciting as it was insightful. Mises' criticisms of other economic schools of thought and of other intellectual traditions subtly combined wisdom and polemic in proportions that carried the listener to the pitch of feverish excitement.

In an absolutely brilliant manner Mises would open the newspaper, choose a so-called modern-day economic problem, and then spend the hour explaining slowly and carefully why it was only a pseudoproblem in disguise. Mises would explain that the alleged problem either consisted of somebody's disapproval of the voluntary choices made by others (and hence was a noneconomic problem) or was the consequence of some fundamental imbalance introduced in the market by prior acts of state intervention. Modern economists sometimes distinguish between ultimate solutions to problems and solutions that, while not permanent, are at the moment politically feasible. Thus, for example, given the fact that modern governments refuse to use monetary deflation as a means of adjusting domestic price levels, economists discuss what second-best alternatives are available. For Mises there was no time to play patch-up games with a failing economy; Mises was interested in the ultimate source of the problem and its ultimate solution. Mises provided his students with a deep understanding of economic policy that often crossed the border into the realm of political philosophy itself.

Above all, Mises presented his students with a "paradigm" that has come to be associated with the work of the Austrian school of economics and in particular the pioneering thought of Carl Menger. According to Mises, and the Austrian school in general, the economic system is a delicate arrangement that coordinates and sometimes synchronizes individual plans without the need for centralized direction and often in spite of cumbersome governmental interventions. The so-called competitive model where individuals are reduced to profit-maximizing calculators not only distorts real world relations but pushes economics into a mold that partially obscures the subjective character of "costs" and "values" and ignores the uncertainties that individual actors experience when formulating their plans. For Mises, economic theory is more than a set of convenient assumptions that permit the systematic arrangement of historical statistics: economics offers insight into the nature of the human condition itself.

My first meeting with Mises occurred when I was nineteen years of age. At the prompting of a best-friend, we boarded the IND subway train in Queens to make the nearly hour-long trek to Manhattan's financial district. There at New York University's School of Business, Mises was holding his economic theory seminar in the early evening hours. The subject of the seminars varied from year to year and ranged from a discussion of socialism to the international monetary mechanism. Toward the end of 1964 I invited Mises to give a talk at my school, Queens College of the City University of New York, on the subject of "Some Epistemological Problems of Economics." Mises agreed to come, and the school newspaper asked me to write a précis of his life and writings so as to publicize his arrival on campus. In my article I recalled my first seminar meeting with Mises and how he "broke the ice" and encouraged all those present not to be in awe of him but to participate in the discussion. Let me conclude this introduction by quoting from my article in Queens College's *Phoenix* (5 January 1965), because it conveys something of Mises "the teacher" that I have neither forgotten nor tired of recalling:

A silence smothered the plushly carpeted room as our professor reached for a copy of the *New York Times*. He began to read from page one. I missed the opening paragraphs—it took a while to adjust to his Austrian-French accent—it was a story about an upcoming meeting of the International Monetary Fund. In essence, they were gathering to discuss the perennial balance of payments problem between their nations. His articulation was slow, deliberate. I knew what he thought of the IMF, and yet his tone showed not one bit of contempt for it. He put down the paper and restated the problem in a manner more comprehensible than the *Times* itself.

Mises' questioning begged an answer. All heads were bowed in thought, and Mises asked if someone would be kind enough to suggest an answer. No one volunteered. Who would dare posit their knowledge against his? In the event a fallacious doctrine might be espoused, would he become as caustic as he was in the past toward his intellectual opponents?

It was obvious that Mises understood that his stature blocked the flow of conversation. For the first time that evening he frowned. Suddenly he spoke, "Please do not be afraid to make a mistake, the greatest mistakes in economics have been made already." He welcomed the laughter followed by wholesome discussion.

I returned many times in the weeks that followed to hear and take part in his economic theory seminar. I read his books and questioned those aspects of his thought with which I disagreed. Oddly enough the more I argued against some of his tenets the more he seemed to appreciate my presence. I slowly began to understand what Mises' philosophy is essentially about. It is more than a theory of economics, and more than a program for political activity. It is a philosophy built around the individual considering his opinions and decisions to be important. Mises' "laissez-faire" is more than a plea for economic sanity—it is a plea for human toleration.

NOTES

1. For bibliographical information on Mises, see Bettina Bien [Greaves], *The Works of Ludwig von Mises* (Irvington-on-Hudson, N.Y.: Foundation for Economic Education, 1969), pp. 3-9; *International Encyclopedia of the Social Sciences*, s.v. "von Mises, Ludwig"; William H. Peterson, "Ludwig von Mises," *Intercollegiate Review* 9 (Winter 1973-74): 37-41; and Murray N. Rothbard, *The Essential von Mises* (Lansing, Mich.: Oakley R. Bramble, 1973). Mises' younger brother Richard von Mises (1883-1953) was the well-known applied mathematician and formulator of the frequency interpretation of probability (*International Encyclopedia of the Social Sciences*, s.v. "von Mises, Richard"). There was a third brother, younger than Ludwig and Richard, who died while still a boy.

2. On the history of the Austrian school and its early members see R. S. Howey, *The Rise of the Marginal Utility: 1870:1889* (Lawrence, Kans.: University of Kansas Press, 1960), pp. 24-27, 139-78. Carl Menger retired from teaching in 1903 to devote himself entirely to his studies. Wieser took over Menger's chair in 1903 and served until 1922. Böhm-Bawerk returned to teach at Vienna in 1905 and served until his death in 1914. Mises was also influenced by Eugen Philippovich, who served on the Vienna faculty from 1893 until his death in 1917 (ibid., p. 162).

3. Ludwig von Mises, *Die Entwicklung des gutsherrlich-bäuerlichen Verhältnisses in Galizien: 1772-1848* (Leipzig: Franz Deuticke, 1902).

4. At the University, Mises taught a variety of courses over the years. They included history of economic thought, monetary theory, and

business cycles. At his office in the Austrian Chamber of Commerce, Mises held a second seminar for his select students and friends where individual reports on recent work were followed by lengthy discussions. Apparently admission to Mises' private seminar was a great honor. Issues ranging from pure economics to the philosophy of science were discussed and debated by such eminent persons as Friedrich Hayek, Fritz Machlup, Oskar Morgenstern, Gottfried Haberler, Gerhard Tintner, Karl Schlesinger, Erich Schiff, Martha Stefanie Braun, Ilse Mintz, Felix Kaufmann, and Alfred Schutz. Mises, together with Hans Mayer, Friedrich Hayek, Fritz Machlup, and Oskar Morgenstern, founded the Austrian Economic Society (Nationalökonomische Gesellschaft), which met one to three times a month. Among the guest speakers were Jacob Viner, Frank Knight, Lionel Robbins, and Frank Graham, to mention only a few of the British visitors to Vienna.

5. See Appendix.

6. See my essay "The Monetary Economics . . .," note 1.

7. See Murray N. Rothbard, *The Essential von Mises*, p. 49. Lionel Robbins, at the London School, was already familiar with the teachings of the Austrian school from having traveled to Vienna and lectured before Mises' group during the twenties (see note 4 above).

8. See Carl Menger, *Problems of Economics and Sociology*, trans. Francis J. Knock (Urbana: University of Illinois Press, 1963). See also Talcott Parsons, "Introduction," in Max Weber's *The Theory of Social and Economic Organization* (Glencoe, Ill.: Free Press, 1964), pp. 8-29.

9. See Appendix B for full citations to these works and the others referred to in the remainder of this section.

10. In Geneva, Mises retained his warm and dedicated interest in the intellectual development of his students. Professor Alexander Kafka recalled several pleasant Sunday afternoon drives, on which economic issues were discussed, and afternoon tea at Mises' apartment to which students were invited. Professor Kafka was an undergraduate at the time, having been sent by his professors at the German University in Prague to study economics at Geneva with Mises.

11. The following individuals, each an academic economist, attended Mises' seminars on a regular basis: Israel M. Kirzner, Laurence S. Moss, William H. Peterson, George Reisman, Murray N. Rothbard, Hans Sennholz, Louis Spadaro, and Leland Yeager. See Appendix A for a listing of Mises' honorary degrees, *Festschriften,* and related subjects.

12. "Ludwig von Mises, Distinguished Fellow, 1969," *American Economic Review* 59 (September 1969): frontispiece.

Opening Remarks:
Mises, Keynes, and the
Question of Influence

Fritz Machlup

One day, many years ago, I received a visit from a Japanese professor, who introduced himself with these strange words: "You are my grand-teacher!" I had not met him before and therefore looked a bit puzzled; he continued, "You see, Professor M. at Kobe University was my teacher, and inasmuch as you were his teacher, you are my grand-teacher." Well, I could have told him that, since Ludwig von Mises was my teacher, Mises was his grand-grand-teacher!

Right now in this meeting room, I suppose there are some grand-grand-students of Ludwig von Mises, several grand-students, and even a few students. I know that, besides myself, Professor Kirzner, Professor Rothbard, and, for some time, Professor Moss were directly taught by Mises. Without making any further search for direct and indirect students of Mises at this gathering, allow me a few observations on intellectual connections between the writings of Mises and those of another great figure in our discipline.

For more than thirty years economists have been under the spell of John Maynard Keynes. Some became violent Keynesians and others violent anti-Keynesians, but, as Milton Friedman has said, in some sense everybody became a Keynesian, even if he rejected some of Keynes' concepts and all of his precepts. You may be in-

9

terested in finding out what Keynes himself wrote about Mises. To what extent, if any, was Keynes a Misesian?

Let me take as my first bit of evidence Keynes' remarks about Mises that appear in the *Treatise on Money*. Keynes wrote as follows:

The notion of the distinction which I have made between Savings and Investment has been gradually creeping into economic literature in quite recent years. The first author to introduce it was, according to the German authorities [and Keynes cited Albert Hahn and Joseph Schumpeter], Ludwig Mises in his *Theorie des Geldes und der Umlaufsmittel* . . . published in 1912.[1]

Later on in his *Treatise* Keynes made the following statement:

More recently a school of thought has been developing in Germany and Austria under the influence of these ideas, which one might call the neo-Wicksell school, whose theory of bank-rate in relation to the equilibrium of Savings and Investment, and the importance of the latter to the Credit Cycle, is fairly close to the theory in this Treatise. I would mention particularly Ludwig Mises's *Geldwertstabilisierung und Konjunkturpolitik* (1928).[2]

In addition, Keynes cited Hans Neisser's *Der Tauschwert des Geldes* (1928) and Friedrich Hayek's *Geldtheorie und Konjunkturtheorie* (1929).[3] Following these citations Keynes added a footnote that is of interest because, although Keynes had already attributed to Mises the novel and original idea of the relationship between saving and investment and had credited him with having discussed its importance to monetary theory, Keynes confessed:

I should have made more references to the work of these writers if their books, which have only come into my hands as these pages are being passed through the press, had appeared when my own thought was at an earlier stage of development, and if my knowledge of the German language was not so poor (in German I can only clearly understand what I know already!—so that *new* ideas are apt to be veiled from me by difficulties of language).[4]

Apparently John Maynard Keynes had forgotten that in 1914, sixteen years earlier, he had reviewed the first German edition of

Mises' *Theory of Money and Credit*. Let me read to you from Keynes' review, which appeared in the *Economic Journal*.

Dr. von Mises' treatise is the work of an acute and cultivated mind. But it is critical rather than constructive, dialectical and not original. . . .Dr. Mises strikes an outside reader as being the very highly educated pupil of a school, once of great eminence, but now losing its vitality. . . .One closes the book . . . with a feeling of disappointment that an author so intelligent, so candid, and so widely read should, after all, help one so little to a clear and constructive understanding of the fundamentals of his subject. . . . When this much has been said, the book is not to be denied considerable merits. Its lucid common sense has the quality, to be found so much more often in Austrian that in German authors, of the best French writing. The treatment throughout is primarily theoretical, and quite without striving after *actualité*. The book is "enlightened" in the highest degree possible.[5]

So you can see how difficult it is to recognize originality when one cannot read the language in which it is expressed!

We shall now be treated to five scholarly discussions of Mises' contributions to economic science and social philosophy. The organizers of this session have done a thoughtful job of dividing the territory—though without any unlawful restraint of trade. We shall first have Professor Laurence Moss appraise Mises' monetary theory. Then Professor Israel Kirzner will present Mises' views on capital theory. They will be followed by Professor Murray Rothbard, talking on Mises' thoughts on economic calculation under socialism, and by Professor William Baumgarth, analyzing Mises' justification of a liberal order of society. These four papers will be subjected to a comprehensive critical scrutiny by Professor Karen Vaughn. I am fortunate in being allowed to preside over such a sympathetic symposium in the memory of our master.

NOTES

1. John Maynard Keynes, *A Treatise on Money* (London: Macmillan & Co., 1930) 1: 171n, in the Royal Economic Society, *The Collected Writings of John Maynard Keynes* (Cambridge: Macmillan & Co.; New York: St. Mar-

tin's Press, 1971) 5: 154n. The work by Mises to which Keynes referred was translated in its second edition and published under the title *The Theory of Money and Credit.* [See Appendix B for complete citation.—Ed.]

2. Keynes, *A Treatise* (1930), p. 199; (1971), p. 178. .

3. Hans Neisser's book has not been translated into English. Friedrich A. Hayek's work was translated by Nicholas Kaldor and H. M. Croome under the title *Monetary Theory and the Trade Cycle* (London: Alden Press, 1933).

4. Keynes, *A Treatise* (1930), p. 199n; (1971), p. 178n.

5. John Maynard Keynes, "Review of *Theorie des Geldes und der Umlaufsmittel* by Ludwig von Mises and of *Geld und Kapital* by Friedrich Bendixen," *Economic Journal,* 24 (September 1914): 417.

The Monetary Economics

of Ludwig von Mises

Laurence S. Moss

The first edition of Ludwig von Mises' *Theory of Money Credit* appeared in 1912, one year after the publication of Irving Fisher's *Purchasing Power of Money* (1911) but more than a decade before Alfred Marshall's *Money, Credit, and Commerce* (1922).[1] Despite the important contributions of Fisher and Marshall to the area of monetary economics, it was Mises who produced the first systematic study of the relationship among money, interest, and prices after Wicksell's celebrated *Interest and Prices* (1898).[2] While Wicksell's, Marshall's, and Fisher's respective contributions are ritualistically consulted by contemporary scholars, Mises' contribution is largely neglected and is no longer considered essential to a mastery of the subject matter of monetary economics. Yet the *Theory of Money and Credit* cannot be described as either an obscure book or one that has failed to influence the development of monetary economics. The list of scholars who have indicated at least some familiarity with Mises' monetary thought is formidable and includes men of acknowledged reputation such as Knut Wicksell, Benjamin Anderson, Lionel Robbins, John Maynard Keynes, John R. Hicks, A. W. Marget, and Don Patinkin. If to this

I wish to thank Professors Leland Yeager and Gerald O'Driscoll for reading an earlier draft of this monograph and making several valuable comments. Naturally they are in no way responsible for the interpretation I present here.

list we add the names of several generations of veteran participants in Mises' famous monetary seminars, offered first in Vienna, then in Geneva, and later in New York, the roster must be expanded to include Friedrich Hayek, Fritz Machlup, Gottfried Haberler, Alexander Kafka, Leland Yeager, Murray Rothbard, Israel Kirzner, and myself, to name only a few.[3]

What is it about this book and the arguments it contains that has kept it for nearly seventy years in limbo between virtual obscurity and academic acclaim? It is my view that Mises' *Theory of Money and Credit* has all the earmarks of a genuine economic classic—it touches on more of the essential problems of monetary economics than any other single work of the first quarter of the twentieth century—but it lacks an acceptable methodological framework for analyzing monetary problems. Where J. R. Hicks, Oscar Lange, and Don Patinkin harnessed the mathematical technique of "mutual determination" to the solution of the fundamental issues in monetary economics, Mises operated in the world of deductive-casual models in the acknowledged tradition of Menger and Böhm-Bawerk. While orthodox monetary theory developed its essential propositions for a world without lags and troublesome distribution effects, Mises put all this at the heart of his analytic system.

I shall illustrate these points by showing how Mises' monetary economics is related to several currents of thought in the period before World War I. In section 1, I begin by critically evaluating the relation of Mises' theory of the demand for money to the work of his mentor and founder of the Austrian school, Carl Menger. I show that by confusing the demand for money with the demand for the *services* provided by money, Mises was forced to modify one of the basic tenets of the Austrian position in order to apply the theory of marginal utility to money. Also, I demonstrate how Mises' insistence on the relative unimportance of the speculative demand for money actually cut short a line of development in Austrian thought that would have proved useful to his own theory of business fluctuations. I conclude by summarizing the important contributions Mises made toward our understanding of the relationship between price expectations and inflation.

In section 2, I treat the influence of Wicksell and Fisher on Mises' monetary thought. More specifically I show how Wicksell's use of "cash balances" to bridge the gap between the commodity and money markets and Fisher's presentation of the quantity equation encouraged Mises (1) to carefully distinguish between accounting prices and money prices and (2) to insist on the importance of "wealth effects" in understanding the impact of changes in the money supply on the economy.

In section 3 I show how the Mises-Hayek theory of the business cycle originated in Mises' attempt to apply his theory of money to the "cumulative expansion" problem raised by Wicksell. A concluding section offers a brief statement of Mises' contribution to monetary policy.

1. THE DEMAND FOR MONEY

For both Menger and Mises, the important fact about money is that it does not come into existence by community vote or governmental fiat but instead is the unintended consequence of the historical evolution of the market economy. Individuals engage in trade and commerce in order to acquire commodities capable of satisfying human wants. They willingly trade commodities only if they expect to improve their situations by doing so. There are circumstances, however, in which an individual may find it profitable to accept a commodity in exchange, not because that commodity is itself directly suited or serviceable to his personal needs but rather because he expects to be able to market that commodity at a later date for other commodities that are directly serviceable to his wants. Such a commodity acts as a medium through which exchange takes place.[4]

In an exchange economy virtually all commodities are marketable, but not to the same extent. As commerce develops, individuals discover that certain commodities are acceptable on many markets; this acceptance establishes their reputation as media of exchange and further enhances their marketability. Eventually one commodity snowballs in reputation and becomes readily acceptable on all markets. This commodity is called "money," and its essential feature is its universal marketability.

The marketability attribute of the money commodity is sometimes confused with its purchasing power, that is, its ability to command a definite quantity of another commodity in exchange. Marketability refers to the frequency with which a commodity is accepted in trade. It is true that this frequency itself must be conditioned by how many units of another commodity this first commodity may be expected to command in exchange, but it is not the extent of the purchasing power of this commodity in *particular* markets that is important in defining "marketability"; rather it is the fact that a commodity is capable of being traded in *all* markets. Stated another way, what is important about money is not that it is a "temporary abode of purchasing power" but that it is a temporary abode of purchasing power in all markets.[5]

In the typical model of the barter economy there can be no a priori way of deciding which of the commodities is best suited to be money, because all commodities are assumed to be traded against one another. One cannot say that it will be the commodity with the greatest purchasing power that will serve as the medium of exchange, because at any set of relative prices one can always make the objective exchange value of a commodity look greater by redefining the units in which it is measured. According to Menger, the "most marketable commodity" is determined as the outcome of a complex historical process, which can be described in only the most general manner. The origin of money is as elusive as the origin of language itself.[6]

While Menger used this historical account merely to explain that the process by which the community comes to adopt one commodity as its money is thoroughly market oriented, Mises attempted to expand the argument so as to account for the determination of the purchasing power of the monetary unit as well. According to Mises, when an individual decides what the size of his nominal, or cash, balances is to be, he consults the purchasing power of money as it appeared "yesterday" in the market. This decision on the part of all individuals about the optimal size of their nominal balances will in turn affect the purchasing power of money "today" and thereby require that individuals readjust their balances "tomorrow," until, according to Mises, an "equilibrium" position is reached.[7] In this way the past behavior of market prices affects future market outcomes.

At first sight, this appears to be a peculiar position for a member of the Austrian school to adopt. Menger and the Austrians that followed him never tired of explaining that the market process is "forward looking" and not imprisoned by the past. Commodities are valued today because they are capable of satisfying future wants, and resources are valued according to the intensity and extent of the future wants they are capable of satisfying. All market prices are ultimately derived from the marginal utilities of the commodities they help produce. In the market "bygones are forever bygones"; that is, while past historical data may guide the market participants in their plans, they never guarantee their successful outcome. Menger, Böhm-Bawerk, and Mises were in agreement that there is no greater fallacy in the entire science of economics than the pernicious doctrine that monetary costs expended on the production of commodities determine what the market prices of those commodities will be. The downfall of the English classical school was its failure to recognize that the value of resources is derived from the value of the commodities they help produce, and any coincidence between cost of production and market price simply indicates that entrepreneurs have been successful at their job of anticipating *future* needs.[8]

It is not necessary to proceed further with this summary of the Austrian theory of value in order to indicate how heretical Mises' position on money may seem to those familiar with the position of the older Austrian school. To assert that the value of money depends on its past purchasing power is to admit that the past behavior of prices exerts an influence on future prices—the very antithesis of Menger's teachings. Let us see by what reasoning Mises came to this position.

We begin by developing Mises' notion of "pure fiat money." As is well known, the commodity that the community adopts as its money generally possesses certain physical characteristics that make it capable of satisfying a variety of nonmonetary wants. For example, gold coins can be melted down to make jewelry, and paper money can be used to wallpaper a room. According to Mises, these other uses of the money commodity outside the sphere of exchange must be considered of secondary importance to a general theory of money. A pure theory of money must yield theorems that apply to all forms of money regardless of the material out of which it is made. Mises explained how the historical evolution of monetary and banking institutions (for example, the development of the clearing system and the introduction of a variety of paper monies into the exchange economy) demonstrates that no fact about money essential to the determination of its purchasing power depends on the stuff out of which the money is made.[9] Thus it is necessary at the outset of any investigation into the pure theory of money to abstract completely from the real-world fact that money is often made of valuable materials that are themselves capable of satisfying nonmonetary wants. The reader may find it useful to think of the entire stock of money as consisting of paper money, with the paper of so poor a quality that it has no alternative use outside the monetary sphere. From now on our use of the term *money* refers to these disembodied units of purchasing power. In Hicks' felicitous phrase, money is the "ghost of gold."[10] The problem then is to explain how individuals decide how many units of money to hold, that is, how they determine the size of their cash balances.

Inasmuch as individuals do find it necessary to hold money and expend part of their wealth in order to acquire money, this disembodied object must satisfy some want. Furthermore, the stock of money in the possession of each individual is capable of variation, as individuals are constantly faced with the choice of building up or reducing their existing cash balances, that is, they are compelled to arrive at an estimate of the marginal utility of money. According to Mises, the marginal utility of money is derived from the marginal utility of the commodities money is capable of purchasing, or, stated another way, the use value of money coincides exactly with its exchange value.[11] It would seem, therefore, that if the demand for money depends entirely on the exchange value of money, individuals must have some idea of what the purchasing power of money is prior to determining the size of their cash balances. But how can individuals have any idea the purchasing power of money when it depends in large part on the size of the cash balances individuals are willing to hold? Thus we seem to have come full circle in our attempt to explain the purchasing power of money by means of utility theory. What we have arrived at is the infamous "circularity problem," which was one of the leading problems in monetary theory at the time Mises wrote.[12]

It will be instructive at this point if we try to understand why this same problem does not arise in an analysis of the exchange value of a nonmonetary commodity such as bread. The marginal utility of bread depends on the physical characteristics of bread that make it serviceable to men's wants and the hierarchy of wants themselves. According to Mises, both sets of conditions do not belong to the "economic at all but are partly of a technological and partly of a psychological nature."[13] Having described the demand conditions for bread, it is in principle possible to determine the exchange value of bread. But with money the situation is altogether different because "the subjective value of money is conditioned by its [purchasing power] i.e., by a characteristic that falls within the scope of economics."[14] In the case of money it is not possible (even "in principle") to conceive of its having value without making reference to its past purchasing power.

We may question whether this distinction between money and other commodities is not a bit overdrawn. There are many commodities that individuals demand partly for their want-satisfying characteristics and partly because they are capable of being exchanged at a later date for other commodities. We need not restrict our examples to rare coins and antiques, inasmuch as all commodities that shed their services over extended periods are capable of being resold during their lifetime in highly developed resale markets. In cases such as these would not the exchange value of the commodity itself affect the market demand? Certainly Mises would be prepared to admit that in a highly developed economy, all commodities, insofar as they yield any liquidity services, could also serve as "assets."

While Mises did not deny the obvious possibility that in an advanced money economy individuals may acquire nonmonetary commodities for the express purpose of being able to exchange them at a later date for other commodities directly serviceable to their needs, he insisted that this practice only becomes widespread during exceptional times, that is, when the existing monetary order is headed for a complete breakdown as during the course of hyperinflation. According to Mises, "Under present organization of the market, which leaves a deep gulf between the marketability of money on the one hand and of other economic goods on the other hand, nothing but money enters into consideration at all as a medium of exchange. Only in exceptional circumstances is any other economic good pressed into this service."[15] Thus when Mises insisted that the marginal utility of commodities is determined by nonmarket considerations and the marginal utility of money is derived entirely from its exchange value, we must interpret this as pertaining to a money economy operating under what Mises described as "ordinary circumstances."

In such an economy individuals find it necessary to hold cash balances because they need to maintain a fund of instant purchasing power. The number of units of money they demand depends on the efficiency of the monetary unit in acquiring commodities, and this in turn depends on the past array of market prices. When planning their cash requirements on a particular market day, individuals have no basis for evaluating the purchasing power of money other than its past "track record." Thus while all other market plans are essentially forward looking in the sense described earlier, the demand for money is necessarily "backward looking." Mises explained that to "demand of a theory of the value of money that it should explain the exchange-ratio between money and [other] commodities solely with reference to the monetary function, and without the assistance of the element of historical continuity in the value of money, is to make demands of it that run quite contrary to its nature and its proper task."[16]

It will be helpful to distinguish between the two following propositions:

1. Since money *qua* money is desired because it is a medium of exchange (and not because of the physical characteristics of the materials out of which it is made), it is impossible to derive a theory of the demand for money consistent with the utility theory of value, which does not make reference to the past behavior of market prices.
2. Individuals when planning the size of their cash balances form expectations about future price behavior on the basis of past price experience.

Both propositions are part of Mises' *Theory of Money and Credit,* but while the first asserts something about the character of analytic constructs in monetary theory, the second is a bold empirical hypothesis of the way individuals behave in a market economy. I shall evaluate Mises' claim about the logical structure of monetary theory first and then return to the use he makes of his empirical hypothesis in his description of the inflationary process.

1. In his assertion that the *only* way the demand for money can be consistently incorporated into the general body of utility theory is by introducing historical prices, Mises is quite mistaken. Patinkin demonstrated how to derive a demand curve for money without resorting to past price behavior by performing what is essentially a "thought experiment" in which the individual is confronted with alternative levels of commodity prices and asked how many units of money he will demand in each case. The set of all combinations of price levels and resulting money demands constitutes the individual demand curve for cash balances. The aggregation of all individual demand curves "horizontally" at all price levels yields the market demand curve for nominal balances, and this in conjunction with the (assumed inelastic) supply of money serves to define the "market-clearing" price level. This procedure is the analogue of the familiar neoclassical supply-and-demand analysis, which serves to define the market-clearing price for particular commodities. In Patinkin's barter-money model there is no reference to past price behavior because the method of

"comparative statistics" abstracts completely from historical time.[17]

It is interesting to notice, however, that Patinkin and Mises agreed that the individual cannot decide the extent of his monetary needs (i.e., the size of his cash balances) without knowledge of the array of market prices. Both writers assumed that the demand for a certain number of units of the money commodity is really a disguised demand for a definite quantity of reserve purchasing power. The individual has no way of determining how many units of money he will require unless he has some knowledge of the absolute effectiveness of each unit in acquiring other commodities in the market. What enters into each individual's utility function is not the demand for a certain quantity of money but the demand for a certain fund of ready purchasing power, what Patinkin appropriately called "real balances."[18]

The introduction of "real balances" as a factor in the utility function is quite congenial to the spirit of Mises' analysis. Mises argued at great length that the money commodity is desired only because of the nonmonetary commodities it is capable of purchasing. Individuals continually adjust the size of their cash balances so that the number of units of money they hold provides them with a certain quantity of purchasing power. If an individual perceives that his cash balances are providing him with a greater amount of purchasing power than he desires, he will buy either interest-bearing securities or commodities in an effort to "dispose of the superfluous stock of money that lies useless on his hands." In the opposite case, where cash balances are too small, the individual will "take steps to reach the desired level of reserve purchasing power by suitable behaviour in making sales and purchases."[19]

Having decided that Mises' demand for money is really a demand for a certain quantity of real cash balances, we ask what determines the size of real cash balances individuals desire to hold? The basic reason for holding money is the lack of simultaneity between payments and receipts and the need to hold transaction balances in order to bridge the gap between the two. Mises reasoned that since money enters into most transactions, in a growing economy, as the number of transactions per person increases, the individual is required to hold larger stocks of real cash balances.[20]

According to Mises, however, the largest part of the real balances held by individuals is used to provide for unplanned expenses that may arise in the future. A sudden illness or an unanticipated breakdown in plant machinery makes it necessary for economic agents to hold a certain quantity of reserve purchasing power as a type of insurance. Mises explained that this precautionary demand for real cash balances, unlike the transactions demand, tends to fall as the market economy develops highly liquid forms of interest-bearing property. The individual holds a precautionary stock of real balances because the transaction costs of moving out of non-monetary assets into money are too great to effectively meet emergency payments. With the development of resale markets for certain types of securities these costs decline substantially, and individuals are thereby able to maintain a certain level of liquidity by substituting securities for real cash balances.[21]

It would seem then that the "premium" the individual pays for the marginal dollar of precautionary balances is measured by the interest forgone by not purchasing a dollar's worth of "highly liquid" securities. But Mises denied this implication by stating that to regard "interest as compensation for the temporary relinquishing of money [is a view of] insurpassable naivety."[22] Elsewhere Mises was even more explicit about this matter when he denied that the demand for *real* cash balances is in any way interest elastic: he wrote that there is no direct connection between the rate of interest and the amount of money held by the individuals who participate in the transactions of the market.[23] Thus while Mises did describe something approximating a liquidity-preference demand for real cash balances, he insisted (without argument) that there is no regular functional relationship between the interest rate and the demand for such balances.

In the end Mises viewed real cash balances as something individuals must hold because of the structure of the payments mechanism and the uncertain nature of the world in which they live. While the size of an individual's real balances is a subjective matter determined by his own appraisal of his economic situation and subject to revision from time to time, the individual views these balances as sort of the dues he must pay in order to successfully participate in the market economy.[24] Certainly they provide the individual with utility but only in the same way that the legal order provides individuals with utility—real balances are merely part of the framework within which market action takes place.

Thus Mises' writings reveal a tendency to view the individual's desired level of real balances as something relatively constant and determined by the structure of the world in which he operates and the way he perceives that world. This approach is actually a retrogression from Menger's concept of the demand for money. In his late writings Menger argued that the bulk of the cash balances are held by individuals for speculative purposes. For Menger, market prices are subject to wide dispersion over both time and place; consequently, individuals hold money balances in search of "bargain prices." For example, an individual seeking to purchase a "used" typewriter must have the ready cash to move into the market for typewriters without delay as soon as he spies a machine being offered on favorable terms. In this way, Menger called attention to the speculative demand for money that applies to all markets wherever future prices are uncertain.[25]

Although the holding of speculative balances means forgoing the opportunity of purchasing an interest-bearing asset, this loss promises to be offset by the marginal capital gain of buying a commodity on more favorable terms than would otherwise be possible. Clearly, a lowering of the market rate of interest must encourage an increased holding of real balances for speculative purposes, and hence the liquidity-preference approach is entirely consistent with Menger's treatment of the demand for money. In Menger's view, the speculative balances held by individuals are a rational response to a world of uncertain prices, and balances held for this purpose are actually a type of investment, the rate of return on which can be measured by the expected capital gain of the individual.

Without explanation Mises simply rejected the Mengerian notion of an investment demand for money except during the exceptional times of monetary crisis. Mises agreed with Menger that during the long evolutionary period before a single money came into existence the competing media of exchange had to be marketable over both time and place. However, with the appearance of highly developed markets for the resale of interest-bearing property, this store-of-value function of money loses importance, as few will demand real cash balances for investment purposes when they can own interest-bearing assets instead. Here Mises simply failed to recognize that from the economic point of view speculative balances are not "barren" but perform a valuable service for the individual.[26]

If it were possible to measure the amount of price variation that characterizes each market in the economy, the resulting "coefficients of price variation" would come out lowest for those markets in which standardized commodities like bread, milk, and other articles of final consumption are sold and highest for the markets in which the industrial ovens for baking bread and the machinery needed to process the milk are sold. What I have in mind here is that capital goods transactions as well as all other transactions that involve other highly specialized goods may offer an opportunity for speculative behavior that does not exist in markets closer to the consumer. If this is true, a lowering of the market rate of interest will produce not only an increased demand for speculative balances but also an increased trade in markets for what Menger called "higher order" goods. This may result in a deepening of the capital structure, something that both Mises and later Hayek described as characteristic of the boom period of the business cycle, when banks encourage borrowing by lowering the market rate of interest. It is unfortunate that Mises overlooked Menger's speculative demand for money and the implied interest elasticity of the demand for real balances, because it really opens a line of investigation that might have proved quite congenial to his own work on the business cycle.[27]

To summarize: Mises explained the individual's demand for real cash balances in terms of both the transactions and precautionary

motives, motives that depend on "the organisation of the whole
social apparatus of production and exchange" and not on either the
interest rate or the individual's own wealth position. Thus while
real cash balances enter into the individual's utility function (as
they must since they are the object of purposive market action),
they enter into it as a fixed magnitude. The individual forms no estimate of the marginal utility of real cash balances but only of the
marginal utility of the monetary unit so that he may decide how
many units of the money commodity he must hold in order to have
some already decided fund of real purchasing power. Patinkin's formulation of the demand for (real) cash balances, which emphasized
the substitution effect between real balances and other forms of
nonmonetary wealth, applies the marginal utility theory directly to
the question of what level of real balances is optimal and hence is a
more general development of the strand of marginal utility analysis
Mises pioneered.[28]

Why did Mises apply the marginal utility theory to the demand
for the money commodity rather than to the demand for real
balances, which the money commodity only represents? I believe
the answer has to do with Mises' unwillingness to include anything
but goods of final consumption in the individual's utility function.[29]
This explains why Mises emphasized that the marginal utility of
money must be defined in terms of the marginal utility of the commodities that money is exchanged for in the market. But in other
places he mentioned the twin services money provides as a bridge
between payments and receipts and as a fund of real purchasing
power against future unforeseen contingencies. Yet it is not enough
that real cash balances are serviceable to wants because they satisfy
them in a manner different from all other commodities. Mises explained that, when an individual destroys, say, one dollar's worth
of milk, the (real) national product falls, but when that same individual burns a dollar's worth of the money commodity, the (real)
national product remains unchanged.[30] Let us elaborate on the
relationships involved here in more detail. The immediate impact
of the destruction of a dollar's worth of money is to lower the in-

dividual's real cash balances by one dollar. If the individual seeks to reestablish his level of real purchasing power, he must consume fewer commodities in the market. This brings about a tendency for market prices to fall just a little, and everyone else's real cash balances to rise just a little. As the other individuals increase their consumption in order to reduce their real cash balances to their desired level, they essentially release the money the first individual is looking for. In equilibrium once again, the stock of money has fallen by one dollar, the price level is a bit lower, but all real magnitudes are left unchanged, including each individual's real cash balances, which have returned to the original level.[31]

Certainly, this suggests that the marginal utility of the money commodity must be zero, since the loss of one unit ultimately results in the loss of nothing real. Mises may well have been troubled by this conclusion, because it implies that individuals seek to acquire something which in the aggregate they really do not want—a position that strikes a sour note among economists who view man as a purposive agent. Had Mises realized that the marginal utility theory should be applied to the *services* provided by real cash balances and not to the money commodity itself, a great deal of obscurity in his discussion might have disappeared. But the year was 1911, and there was much more that had to be said before J. R. Hicks could at last clarify the distinction between the demand for money and the demand for the services provided by money in his famous 1935 article.[32]

Thus we have seen that Mises' statements about the *form* the utility theory must take when applied to the demand for money are largely incorrect and result from a failure to distinguish adequately between the "utility of money" and the "utility of the services provided by money." Patinkin's technique of counting real balances as a part of the individual's wealth, and thereby incorporating real balances directly into the individual's utility function, permits the development of a theory of the demand for money that is not related to historical prices. But while Patinkin's approach offers much in the way of generality, something is also lost. In the Patinkin barter-money model the money commodity can be any of

the many commodities available, since all commodities are assumed to be freely tradable in all markets. The barter economy
is transformed into a money economy by the deceptively simple
assumption that "the nth commodity is money." In the Mises formulation, however, the whole point of the analysis is to explain the
exchange value of a commodity that is different from all others
because it is freely tradable on all markets. Whether the gains in
historical realism offered by Mises' approach are worth the
sacrifice of the theoretical compactness of Patinkin's approach and
whether the two approaches can be combined are questions worth
discussing, especially in light of Clower's criticisms of the barter-
model approach.[33] I shall not stop to consider this problem here.

2. One of the principal contributions of the *Theory of Money and
Credit* is the consistency with which Mises explored the implications
of the fact that individuals consult the past behavior of market
prices when planning the current size of their cash balances. Here
historical prices are used to develop a bold empirical hypothesis
about the way expectations about future prices are formed. In this
area I consider Mises' contributions to be of great doctrinal importance.

Mises employed the hypothesis that the past behavior of prices
affects current planned cash holdings to explain why, in countries
where inflation has been most rapid, "the decrease in the value of
the money has occurred faster than the increase in its quantity."[34]
What happens, according to Mises, is that people come to expect
the inflation to continue well into the future and, rather than have
the purchasing power of their cash balances steadily erode, take actions to reduce their real cash reserves. This causes the inflation to
accelerate as large numbers of individuals go about substituting
commodities and securities for cash. It remained for later
economists to develop a theory of the "optimal" demand for real
cash balances at each level of inflation, but Mises was certainly one
of the early developers of this line of thought.[35]

Mises was also one of the earliest to explain why during prolonged inflations individuals experience a definite "shortage of

money" when it is actually an "abundance of money" that is caus-
ing the inflation in the first place. What happens is that the individuals (anticipating an increase in the *rate* of inflation) allow
their real cash balances temporarily to fall below their (long-run)
desired level. In such circumstances the prices being asked and bid
for most commodities are no longer related to the present quantity
of money in circulation but to the future expected quantity of
money. Individuals allow their cash balances to fall dangerously
low in the expectation that their future money incomes will rise by
enough to allow them to restore their cash balances to the desired
level. If the monetary authorities suddenly lower the growth rate of
the money supply, money incomes will not increase quickly enough
to restore cash balances, and individuals will experience a definite
shortage of money. They will complain to the monetary authorities
about a lack of liquidity and will insist that all would be well if the
monetary authorities would pursue a less restrictive policy. The inability of bankers to understand the causes of this shortage-of-
money phenomenon soon leads them down the perilous path of
stepping up the growth rate of the money supply.[36]

Mises also applied his price-expectations hypothesis to the
problem of "sellers inflation" and sketched an argument that is especially interesting in light of the current economic confrontations
of a cartelized world economy. Mises explained that the modern
economy is characterized by a wide variety of markets in which
cartels, trusts, monopolies, and state-regulated prices predominate.
Ordinarily, the profit-maximizing monopolist discovers the maximum price he can charge by raising his price and watching what
happens to his sales. If sales fall off by enough to lower total
receipts, the monopolist knows that he has gone too far. But during
a prolonged inflation the buyers find it more economical to pay the
higher price asked than to abstain and chance paying a still higher
price later. In Mises' words, buyers pay the higher prices in the
hope of "screwing up" the prices of the goods they sell by enough to
offset the difference. Thus the result is that market demand curves
become more inelastic, and cash balances are reduced to raise the
extra revenues. Thus the inflation indirectly leads to an increase in

the monopoly power of existing cartels and creates the incentives for other cartels to be formed. This argument is an interesting one and may explain why the cartelization of industry and prolonged inflation are not separate events coincidently occurring at the same point in time but rather interconnected phenomena.[37]

While the tendency among economists of Mises' day was to link the demand for cash balances to the current level of economic activity and then bring price expectations in as a sort of afterthought, Mises placed the past behavior of prices at the very heart of his conception of money. The hypothesis that the past behavior of price is the basis on which market participants form their expectations about future price behavior has proved extremely valuable in the econometric investigation of the demand for money, especially during severe inflations.[38] I do not think that Mises has been given adequate credit for having pioneered this approach.[39]

2. THE PROPORTIONALITY THEOREM

There is an affinity between Wicksell's *Interest and Prices* and Mises' *Theory of Money and Credit* because both economists attempted to put the quantity theory on a firm basis by reconciling it with the then-recent marginal utility theory of value.[40] According to Wicksell, the marginal utility theory explains the structure of relative commodity prices but not the absolute level level of the prices themselves. The quantity theory, on the other hand, specifies the price level that is consistent with a given stock of money, volume of output, and "velocity of circulation," but does not explain the mechanism by which changes in the supply of money bring about changes in the level of prices. Wicksell resolved these difficulties by emphasizing the pivotal role cash balances play in linking the money and commodity markets. Every individual is required to hold a certain quantity of (real) money balances in order to conduct his ordinary economic affairs, and when his existing cash balances exceed (or fall short of) this required level, he must expand (or contract) his commodity purchases accordingly. This same behavior carried out simultaneously by large numbers of economic agents results in movements in the absolute level of commodity prices. In the event the money supply increases and (real) cash balances are larger than individuals desire them to be, the increased spending in the commodity market will raise the level of prices and lower real balances until the community is willing to hold the expanded stock of money. When actual (real) cash balances are once again equal to desired (real) cash balances for all individuals, the equilibrium level of prices has been attained.[41]

There can be little doubt that Mises' own presentation of the cash-balance mechanism owed much to Wicksell. However, what disturbed Mises most about Wicksell's presentation of the cash-balance mechanism was his conclusion that the price level generally changes in direct proportion to changes in the quantity of money. What we shall call the "proportionality theorem" is based on the following reasoning: Since, in equilibrium, relative commodity prices are equivalent to the relative marginal utilities of the commodities whose prices are being compared, changes in the size of individual cash balances cannot affect relative prices unless they in some way alter the underlying marginal utilities for the goods in question. Furthermore, the marginal utility of commodities depends entirely on the relationship among the physical characteristics of commodities, their supply, and the hierarchy of human needs, and so alterations in cash holding that do not affect these underlying real magnitudes must leave relative marginal utilities unaltered. Thus when a monetary disturbance has finally worked itself out, all relative prices must be at their original values, which implies that if prices have changed, they must have changed in the same proportion. Said another way, Wicksell argued that changes in the quantity of moeny have a *neutral* impact on relative commodity prices.[42]

Mises flatly denied that there was any way by which the *physical* quantity of money could be increased and relative commodity prices remain unaltered. According to Mises, even if it were possible by some magically defined formula to distribute a given increase in the money supply among individuals in such a way as to leave their relative wealth positions unaltered, demand curves still would not shift to the right by enough to raise prices proportionally. According to Mises, for this shift to occur, the marginal utility schedule of the money commodity must be a rectangular hyperbola so that, say, a doubling of the individual's cash balances lowers the marginal utility of the monetary unit by one-half. Mises dismissed this possibility by stating that it is an "absurdity" to assume that for each individual a doubling of money leads to a halving of the exchange value he ascribes to each unit.[43]

What Mises evidently failed to realize is that this allegedly absurd assumption is implicit in his own account of the demand for money. If the individual demands a certain fund of real purchasing power and continually adjusts his nominal cash balances with this object in mind, then a doubling of his nominal balances will result in a halving of the marginal utility of the monetary unit. To escape this conclusion Mises would have to assume that the individual's demand for real cash balances is itself a variable subject to utility calculations. Then a doubling of the individual's nominal money balances would have the immediate effect of making him wealthier, which probably would increase his demand for *real* balances and prevent the marginal utility of the money commodity from falling by a full one-half.[44] But this approach requires that we include real balances within the individual's utility function, something that, as we have seen, Mises was not willing to do.

Mises also erred when he assumed that Wicksell's "proportionality theorem" *necessarily* requires that the marginal utility of the money commodity be inversely proportional to the size of the individual's nominal cash holdings. As Patinkin elegantly demonstrated for an economy where everyone's wealth position is permanently fixed, all that is required for a given increase in the money supply to lead to a proportional increase in prices is a positive excess demand for each commodity in each market *until* its price has finally doubled. This condition includes the situation Mises described as a special case.[45]

Mises was on more solid ground when he argued that as a *practical matter* an increase in the *physical quantity* of money alters the existing distribution of community wealth and hence cannot have the neutral effect on relative commodity prices that Wicksell and other advocates of the proportionality theorem supposed it would. In this context Mises criticized Irving Fisher for basing part of his defense of the proportionality theorem on a subtle confusion between a change in the physical quantity of money and a change in the accounting definition of the money unit. As Fisher explained in *Purchasing Power of Money,* when the government changes the denomination of money so that what was previously called a "half dollar" is now called a "dollar," all market prices change in the same proportion. Fisher claimed that this is an instance where a doubling of the nominal quantity of money is accompanied by a doubling of all money prices.[46] Mises explained, however, that only the accounting definition of the monetary unit has been changed, not the actual quantity of money. If tomorrow the Bureau of Weights and Measures decrees that all one-inch units are to be renamed "one foot," and all twelve-inch rulers renamed "four yards," and so on, only a fool would insist that the absolute size of all real objects has increased. Changes in the accounting definition of money are of a purely legal, or stipulative, nature and do not necessitate a process of market adjustment.[47]

In Mises' view, every increase in the physical quantity of the money commodity must manifest itself as an increase in the cash balances of one or more economic agents in the market. For this reason, a successful reformulation of the quantity theory must begin with the brute fact that an injection of new money into the economy always results in an increase in the cash balances of certain individuals and never in the cash balances of everyone at once. According to Mises, the economic consequences of this phenomenon necessarily give rise to a redistribution of wealth and hence to an alteration in relative commodity prices. Suppose (under a fiat standard) the monetary authorities print a new batch of money to pay for the completion of a highway project. The members of society directly involved in the highway project find their cash balances greater than they expected and go out to spend the new money on commodities and various financial assets.[48] This increased expenditure brings about a tendency for prices to rise, especially the prices of products favored by the recipients of the new money. However, the money that is spent shows up as an increase in the cash balances of other individuals, and the rise in prices spreads to other commodities. This inflationary process continues and reduces the real balances of individuals *but not to the same extent.* Individuals "weigh" the impact of a change in relative prices differently, and hence some individuals will judge the decline in the purchasing power of money to be very great, while others may view it as being quite small. The more heterogeneous the consumption patterns of individuals (i.e., the wider the currency area), the less reliable will be any single "price index" as a measure of the decline in the purchasing power of the money commodity.[49] When a new equilibrium "price level" is finally attained, the now larger stock of money will be distributed among the market agents in such a way that each is holding his desired level of real purchasing power in the form of cash balances once again. In this new equilibrium position those individuals who were the first to receive the new money (i.e., the highway people) will probably find their wealth positions increased, and those who were the last to receive the new money will probably find their wealth positions worsened. What has happened is that the increase in the quantity of money has given rise to a process of market adjustment that has altered the relative wealth positions of individuals.[50]

It may happen that when relative and absolute prices change so as to make all economic agents once again content with the size of their cash balances, the shift in wealth ends up favoring those individuals with high propensities to save. Secondary effects will be promoting the accumulation of capital, lowering the "natural" rate of interest, and augmenting the productive capacity of the nation. In this way an increase in the quantity of money brings about an increase in production—the well-known phenomenon of "forced savings." But it is just as likely that the increase in the quantity of money could result in "forced consumption" and the destruction of productive capacity. Mises contended that in most cases the phenomena involved are too complex for the monetary authorities to know in advance which tendency will prevail. The only thing that may be said for certain is that some redistribution will occur.[51]

Mises correctly pointed out that the fundamental cause of these elusive "distribution effects" is the lack of simultaneity among various price changes. Those individuals who find their revenues increasing more quickly than their expenses are made wealthier while those in the reverse situation are made poorer. Mises explained (citing Fisher and Knies) that, if it were possible to fully anticipate the extent of the future decrease in the purchasing power of money, these wealth effects could be mitigated by altering contractual interest rates to include an "extra" compensation for the decline in the purchasing power of money. According to Mises, this does happen over short periods as the market rate of interest is observed to move upward during inflations.[52] Over a long period, however, it is difficult if not impossible for individuals to anticipate what impact changes in the purchasing power of money will have on personal standards of welfare.

It is worth mentioning that contemporary discussions of "real indebtedness effects" support Mises' contention that "once-and-for-all" type increases in the quantity of money will have nonneutral effects on the money economy. In a world where it is possible to convert transitory gains into permanent gains by buying and selling bonds, an increase in the quantity of money will not only alter relative commodity prices but will change the real rate of return on capital as well.[53] The "proportionality theorem" still has a place in contemporary monetary theory as a long-run proposition about the relationship between money and prices during prolonged, and therefore anticipated, inflations. Consider the situation where the money supply grows during each period by a certain fixed percentage. According to the standard analysis, after a transitional period during which desired real balances are reduced and long-term contracts "indexed," prices will rise continuously at the same rate as the money supply. The "new" money flows through the economy augmenting individual cash balances by enough to keep their real value constant, and the inflationary revenue that the money-issuing authorities receive is equal to the nominal value of the new money issued.[54] Much discussion has centered on the question of whether the benefits of inflationary finance exceed the burdens imposed on the economic community, but little discussion has focused on the problem Mises raised of the mechanism of market adjustment that these long-run consequences are supposed to follow.

In a world where individual cash balances simply grow in size automatically (like Frank Knight's famous Crusonia Plant), the "proportionality theorem" would have some validity, inasmuch as the new money would never change hands and hence would never give rise to a lagged process of adjustment. But in a world where the money-issuing authorities introduce the new money by buying different types of goods, services, and financial assets (and at different points in time as well), the "first round" of monetary expansion affects the cash balances of individuals differently. To dramatize this point, let us consider the existence of just one individual named Miser Joe whose demand for real balances is infinitely elastic. If new money is given to Miser Joe, the process stops dead in its tracks, despite the fact that the percentage increase in the money supply may be the same in this period as it was in the preceding period. It seems that analysis of fully anticipated inflation requires not only that the rate of growth of money remain fixed but also that the route by which the new money enters and passes through the system stay the same from one period to the next. How this assumption is at all relevant to the historical process by which new money is injected into the economy by existing governments is a point that has not received adequate attention by contemporary theorists.

3. THE ORIGIN OF THE AUSTRIAN THEORY OF THE BUSINESS CYCLE

We have seen that the essence of Mises' approach to monetary economics consists of the view that not only the size of the increase in the money supply but also the route by which the new money enters and makes its way through the economic system affect the final market outcome. It was in applying this method of analysis to a problem raised by Wicksell's famous theory of cumulative expansion that Mises laid the foundations of the Austrian theory of the trade cycle.

In Wicksell's analysis of bank credit expansion, the commercial banks by holding the market rate of interest below the real rate of interest bring about a cumulative increase in the demand for bank loans and consequently a cumulative increase in commodity prices. The problem Wicksell raised in *Interest and Prices* is whether there is an automatic "brake" on the process of bank credit expansion that would prevent the rise in prices from going on indefinitely if the bank authorities keep the market rate of interest below the natural rate and are willing to meet all demands for credit. Wicksell argued that the process of credit expansion must come to a halt when the reserve-deposit ratio of the commercial banks falls below the legal limit or simply becomes too low for the bankers' own comfort. The banks, fearing either "fines" or a full-scale liquidity crisis, raise the money rate of interest, and the inflation comes to a halt with absolute prices remaining permanently higher. In the case of a pure fiat system in which there are no required reserves or convertibility pledges to worry about, the cumulative expansion of the money supply and subsequent inflation can continue as long as the bankers keep the money rate of interest below the real rate of interest.[55]

Mises found Wicksell's analysis of the problem unsatisfactory, and in the third part of his *Theory of Money and Credit* he tried to explain why the cumulative expansion process must come to an end *even under a pure fiat system.*[56] According to Mises, when the commercial banks encourage additional borrowing by lowering the market rate below its natural level, entrepreneurs are encouraged to make more long-term investments, that is, to lengthen the "period of production."[57] With the newly issued bank money entrepreneurs bid resources out of the production of consumption goods into the production of capital goods despite the fact that no additional planned savings has taken place. Consumer prices must rise to generate the "forced savings" required to make the increased capital goods construction possible. Finding wages and resource costs higher than expected, the entrepreneurs turn to the banks to demand a larger quantity of money than before. Mises believed that the size of the money supply would increase not only absolutely but proportionately as well, so that the Wicksellian cumulative expansion process could not go on indefinitely without a collapse of the monetary order under the strains of hyperinflation.[58] The only alternative to the destruction of the monetary order is for the banks to restore equality between the money rate of interest and the natural rate of interest, in which case the sudden cutoff of entrepreneurial loans will require the liquidation of partly completed projects and the transfer of resources to other parts of the economy.[59]

The details of the theory are sketchy, and Mises failed to prove that the rate of growth of the money supply must necessarily accelerate when the market rate is held below the natural rate. It remained for Mises' student F. A. Hayek to develop Mises' idea into a full-fledged theory of the modern trade cycle.[60] The Mises-Hayek theory of the business cycle centers around the idea that the route by which newly created money enters the economy is essential in determining its impact on the monetary order. The analysis treats increases in the quantity of money as necessarily involving changes in relative prices and transfers in wealth among individuals. If present-day monetary economics seems far removed from the concerns of Mises and Hayek, the only reason is that it treats all increases in the quantity of money as being essentially alike and disregards the question of the "transmission mechanism" by which the new money makes its impact felt on the money economy by assuming relative prices are (after a brief transition period) left unchanged.

4. CONCLUSION

Having come to the end of my survey of the monetary economics of Ludwig von Mises, I would like to say a few words about his contribution to the theory of economic policy. Mises favored an international monetary mechanism that would constrain the money-issuing proclivities of modern governments. He recognized that one of the great threats to the liberal ideal of a free, mobile, and prospering world economy is the tendency on the part of government to increase state coffers by using the "printing press' rather than by borrowing or issuing new taxes. For Mises the guaranteed consequence of this policy, which he termed "inflationism," is the wholesale redistribution of the wealth and property of individual citizens. This redistribution is accomplished, not by the method of parliamentary debate and legislative action, but by haphazard and cruel method that leave the poorest and most disadvantaged segments of the population worse off than before. In Mises' view the great threat to the survival of democratic ideals and the organization of modern industrial life is a hyperinflation that would ravage the world economy like an angry fire, destroying the property and aspirations of the masses and creating conditions for military takeover and total state control.[61]

As a practical matter, Mises favored commodity gold standard whereby each government would have to maintain the convertibility of money in terms of gold. Any policy of inflationism would be short lived in the wake of declining gold reserves, or the state would suffer the diplomatic embarrassment of having to redefine its currency unit in terms of gold. Mises, of course, realized that the resource costs of such a monetary arrangement are high, and the system itself is never totally insured against sudden and sometimes massive changes in the quantity of money that originate from, say, technological innovations in the processing of gold or new mine discoveries.[62] But the virtue of the arrangement is not that it eliminates monetary disturbances altogether, but rather that it makes it too costly for the size and growth of the money supply to become an object of government policy. Mises preferred the impersonal mechanisms of the market, no matter how imperfect, to the whims and gluttonous excesses of power-hungry politicians. In Mises' view, the strategy that is currently favored in liberal quarters, that of moving toward a less expensive fiat currency system while urging the monetary authorities to pass parliamentary decrees limiting their own appetites, is as idealistic as expecting a child not to eat candy placed in his hand.

Following Wicksell, Mises called attention to the fact that commercial banks issue deposits that act as a substitute for currency in the cash balances of individuals.[63] According to Mises, the specific way by which banks create money under fractional reserve arrangements and the manner in which they introduce the new money into the economic system necessarily bring about an overinvestment of resources in capital goods production and the need for subsequent business readjustments. For this reason, Mises paired his advocacy of the gold standard with a system of free (competitive) banking in order to eliminate the possibility of severe business downturns.[64]

By modern-day standards Mises must be termed a "monetarist," for he surely believed that changes in the quantity of money are the primary cause of aggregate instability. In one respect, however, Mises was even more radical in his monetarism than traditional advocates of the quantity theory, such as Wicksell, Fisher, and Friedman; for he refused to consider the "proportionality theorem" as being at all relevant to the experiences of modern money economies. The proportionality theorem suggests that there are circumstances in which changes in the quantity of money can lead to changes in the absolute level of commodity prices but leave all real economic magnitudes (i.e., relative prices) unchanged. For Mises there are no circumstances in which the modern technology of money creation permits it to have a neutral impact on the money economy. In short, not only does money matter, but it matters all the time!

NOTES

1. The first edition of Ludwig von Mises' *Theory of Money and Credit* appeared in German in 1912 under the title *Theorie des Geldes und der Umlaufsmittel*. The second German edition appeared in 1924 and included two previously published articles, one on the classification of monetary

theories and the other on the policy of postwar (World War I) deflation. In 1934 the second German edition was translated into English by H. E. Batson and published under the title *The Theory of Money and Credit*, with an introduction by Lionel Robbins (London: Jonathan Cape, 1934). In 1953 a new English edition included an essay "Monetary Reconstruction" (New Haven: Yale University Press, 1953). Mises' writings on monetary theory, inflation, and the trade cycle appeared in a number of other places as well; see Bettina Bien [Greaves], *The Works of Ludwig von Mises* (Irvington-on-Hudson, N. Y.: Foundation for Economic Education, 1969), esp. p. 57. Three important monographs by Mises on monetary questions written between 1923 and 1931 are in the process of being translated. The first monograph, entitled *Geldwertstabilisierung und Konjunkturpolitik* (Jena: Gustav Fischer, 1928), is of special interest because here Mises elaborated on the process by which bank credit expansion distorts relative prices and brings about the conditions of economic crisis. This mechanism is only touched on in his *Theory of Money and Credit* (see my discussion, section 3). The second monograph, *Die Ursachen der Wirtschaftskrise: Ein Vortrag* (Tübingen: J. C. B. Mohr, 1931), criticized the antidepression policies at the time of the Great Depression. The third monograph, *Die Geldtheoretische Seite des Stabilisierungsproblems* (Leipzig: Duncker & Humblot, 1923), applied the theory of monetary inflation to the events leading up to the collapse of the German mark. With these exceptions and another regarding his theory of interest (see note 57 below), Mises did not alter his position or significantly change his formulation of any of the main topics discussed in this paper, so that his entire monetary economics was essentially intact in the 1912 volume. All references in this paper are to the 1953 English edition.

Irving Fisher's *Purchasing Power of Money* first appeared in New York in 1911, and this is the edition to which Mises referred. I shall cite the revised edition of Fisher's book; it appeared in 1913 and was reprinted (New York: Augustus Kelley, 1963). Alfred Marshall's *Money, Credit and Commerce* appeared in London in 1923 and was reprinted (New York: Augustus Kelley, 1965).

2. Knut Wicksell, *Geldzins und Guterpreise* (Jena: Gustav Fischer, 1898) trans. R. F. Kahn, with an introduction by Bertil Ohlin, under the title *Interest and Prices: A Study of the Causes Regulating the Value of Money* (London: Royal Economic Society, 1936). The 1936 translation also contains a reprint of Wicksell's 1907 lecture "The Enigma of Business Cycles," translated by Carl Uhr. All references in this paper are to the reprint of the 1936 edition of *Interest and Prices* (New York: Augustus Kelley, 1962).

3. From 1934 until 1940, when he immigrated to the United States, Mises served as professor of international economic relations at the Institut Universitaire de Hautes Études Internationales in Geneva,

Switzerland. In 1945 Mises was named visiting professor at the Graduate School of Business Administration of New York University; he remained there until his retirement in 1969. For additional biographical information, see my introduction.

4. Cf. Carl Menger, *Principles of Economics*, trans. James Dingwell and Bert F. Hoselitz, with introduction by Frank H. Knight (Glencoe, Ill.: Free Press, 1950), pp. 226-85; and Mises, *Theory of Money*, pp. 30-37.

5. The Austrians themselves were not always clear about the distinction between "purchasing power" and "marketability"; see, for example, Menger, *Principles,* pp. 241-42. The importance of this distinction was argued by R. W. Clower in "A Reconsideration of the Microfoundations of Monetary Theory," *Western Economic Journal* 10 (December 1967): 1-8.

6. Menger, *Principles,* pp. 357-71. Cf. Friedrich A. Hayek, *The Counter-Revolution of Science: Studies on the Abuse of Reason* (Glencoe, Ill.: Free Press, 1955), pp. 82-83.

7. Mises, *Theory of Money*, pp. 111-14. Cf. Wicksell's contribution discussed in section 2.

8. See, for example, Menger, *Principles,* pp. 145-48, 157-61; see also Mises, "Remarks on the Fundamental Problem of the Subjective Theory of Value," *Epistemological Problems of Economics* (Princeton: D. Van Nostrand, 1960), pp. 167-82.

9. Mises distinguished between the juristic and the economic points of view and insisted that demand deposits and bank notes are *money* because they perform the economic function of money regardless of whether or not they have commodity backing (*Theory of Money*, pp. 275-77). On the evolution of banking practices and the substitution of "fiat" for commodity money, see *Theory of Money*, pp. 297-338. Cf. Wicksell, *Interest and Prices*, pp. 62-80.

10. Hicks introduced this phrase in order to ridicule the Misesian concept of money because it tried to offer a historical explanation for the value of the money commodity (see discussion below); for our purposes, however, Hicks's phrase may be used to dramatize how advanced Mises' notion of money actually was for its time (J. R. Hicks, "A Suggestion for Simplifying the Theory of Money," *Economica* 2nd. ser., 2 February 1935 : 1-19; reprinted in Friedrich A. Lutz and Lloyd W. Mints *Readings in Monetary Theory* [Homewood, Ill.: 1951] pp. 14., Cf. Mises' criticism of Wicksell's cumulative process, section 3 below.

11. See, for example, Mises, *Theory of Money*, pp. 109, 119.

12. By using "yesterday's" prices to explain the current demand for money and thereby "today's" prices, Mises is open to the charge of explaining prices by means of prices and hence arguing in a circle. Mises, aware of this objection, developed what he termed the "regression

theorem" to explain how past values could be consistently introduced into a theory of the value of money without arguing in a circle. Mises explained that when we regress and explain "today's" prices by "yesterday's" and "yesterday's" by the "day-before-yesterday's," and so on, we ultimately come to a point in the past when the earliest form of the money commodity emerged. At this time, money took the form of a marketable commodity valued entirely for its nonmonetary uses. Here its market (objective) value was the outcome of the interaction between its supply and the hierarchy of human wants. At this point the historical regression stopped because in principle past price behavior is not needed to determine the market value of this commodity since it has not emerged as "money." Thus Mises' regression theorem states that any object presently used as money is ultimately linked to some commodity that was originally directly serviceable to men's wants, and furthermore, if this link did not exist, society (the collection of valuing minds) would have no epistemological basis for estimating the exchange value of money. The obvious implication of this theorem is that government, no matter how powerful, cannot introduce an object as money unless it first defines that object in terms either of a money already existing or of a commodity whose market value is already established. Once defined in this way, the value of the money commodity eventually (over time) comes to be governed by the behavior of historical prices, and its nonmonetary uses take on a subordinate and sometimes insignificant role (Mises, *Theory of Money*, pp. 120-23). On the circulatrity problem, see Patinkin, *Money, Interest*, pp. 114-16, 573-75. Cf. Mises' discussion of pre-World War I literature in *Theory of Money*, pp. 114-22.

13. Mises, *Theory of Money, p. 97*.

14. Ibid.

15. Ibid, p. 135. Cf. Menger's discussion of commodities as assets (*Principles*, pp. 241-56).

16. Mises, *Theory of Money*, p. 120.

17. Patinkin, *Money, Interest*, pp. 3-43.

18. Ibid, p. 17.

19. Mises, *Theory of Money*, pp. 134-35. Cf. Wicksell, *Interest and Prices*, pp. 39-40; and Patinkin's remark on the significance of this passage in *Money, Interest*, pp. 581-82.

20. Mises explained how, with the development of deposit banking, the larger part of these transaction balances is held in the form of checking accounts (*Theory of Money*, pp. 132, 302-5). On the historical increase in transactions demand for money, Mises wrote, "The characteristic feature of the development of the demand for money is its intensification; the growth of division of labour and consequently of exchange transactions, which have constantly become more and more indirect and dependent on the use

of money . . ." (ibid. p. 151). Mises criticized those who maintain that the transactions demand for money is proportional to the volume of transactions, anticipating Baumol's inventory model by many years.

21. "Every economic agent is obliged to hold a stock of the common medium of exchange sufficient to cover his probable business and personal requirements" (Mises, *Theory of Money*, p. 132). Later Mises wrote, "The uncertainty of the future makes it seem advisable to hold a larger or smaller part of one's possessions in a form that will facilitate a change from one way of using wealth to another, or transition from the ownership of one good to that of another, in order to preserve the opportunity of being able without difficulty to satisfy urgent demands that may possibly arise in the future for goods that will have to be obtained by way of exchange. So long as the market has not reached a stage of development in which all, or at least certain, economic goods can be sold (i.e. turned into money) at any time under conditions that are not too unfavourable, this aim can be achieved only by holding a stock of money of suitable size" (ibid., pp. 147-48).

22. Ibid., p. 353. In an accompanying note Mises identified Law, Cieszkowski, Proudhon, and Macleod as subscribing to this view. According to Hicks, the liquidity preference theory is original with Keynes (*A Treatise on Money*, 2 vols. [London: Macmillan & Co., 1930]) and is the essence of Hicks own suggestion for simplifying the theory of the demand for money (*A Suggestion*, p. 16). Hicks overlooked Menger's contribution to the subject; see my discussion in section 1.

23. Mises, *Theory of Money*, p. 346; see also pp. 148, 350. In these passages Mises referred to the "natural rate" of interest or the real rate of return on capital. At another point in his discussion he admitted that, as bond prices rise, individuals may increase their demand for cash balances, which is equivalent to saying that there is an inverse relationship between the money rate of interest and desired cash balances (ibid., p. 143). What Mises apparently wished to say is that while a temporary change in the demand for cash balances could lead to a change in the money rate of interest, an interest-elastic demand for money could not exist in the long run because there are automatic market forces that will bring the money rate into line with the natural rate (see section 3). There could, however, be an indirect relationship between money and interest through the creation (or destruction) of capital (see section 2).

24. Mises nowhere stated this exactly; but the notion that an individual continually reassesses his need for real cash balances in light of day-to-day-changes in market conditions seems alien to Mises' discussion. He did at one point, however, hint that the demand for real balances may be partly dependent on the individual's wealth position, which does suggest a

modern view of the subject. Mises wrote, "Every separate economic agent maintains a stock of money that corresponds to the extent and intensity with which he is able to express his demand for it in the market" (*Theory of Money*, p. 207). See also discussion, ibid., p. 150.

25. For this interpretation of Menger, I am indebted to Erich W. Streissler, "Menger's Theories of Money and Uncertainty—A Modern Interpretation," in *Carl Menger and the Austrian School of Economics*, ed. J. R. Hicks and W. Weber (Oxford: Clarendon Press, 1973), pp. 164-89. Streissler's discussion of Menger's view on the speculative demand for money was based on an article entitled "Geld," which Menger contributed to *Handwörterbuch der Staatswissenschaften;* it was reprinted in *The Collected Works of Carl Menger*, ed. Friedrich A. Hayek (London: London School of Economics and Political Science, 1936) 4: 1-124. The article went through several editions between 1891 and 1909, the time when Mises was attending the University of Vienna, yet, apparently, Mises did not notice the argument.

26. Mises wrote that "hoarding   cash   as a form of investment no great part in our present stage of economic development, its place having been taken by the purchase of interest-bearing property" (*Theory of Money*, p. 35).

27. Menger denied the relevance of an "equilibrium market price" completely; see Streissler, "Menger's Theories of Money," p. 169. I think it more in keeping with later Austrian thought to deny its relevance to "capital goods" type transactions: see ibid., pp. 171-89. Cf. Donald A. Nichols, "Market Clearing for Heterogeneous Capital Goods," *Micreoconomic Foundations of Employment and Interest Theory*, ed. Edmund S. Phelps et al. (New York: W. W. Norton & Co., 1970), pp, 394-410.

28. Patinkin, *Money, Interest*, pp. 78-116; and esp. pp. 574-75.

29. See discussion in Mises, *Theory of Money*, pp. 79-90.

30. Mises wrote somewhat mysteriously, "The laws which govern the value of money are different from those which govern the value of consumption goods. All that these have in common is their general underlying principle, the fundamental Economic Law of Value" (ibid., p. 86).

31. Our analysis has conveniently ignored "distribution effects," which Mises claimed accompany *all* monetary disturbances of any magnitude: see section 2. Cf. Milton Friedman, *The Optimum Quantity of Money and Other Essays* (Chicago: Aldine Publishing Co., 1969), pp. 14-15.

32. See note 10 above.

33. See note 5 above for reference to Clower's work.

34. Mises, *Theory of Money*, p. 227.

35. Mises believed that "a money which continually fell in value would have no commercial utility," that is, the money would cease to be money

(ibid).This position is false on both empirical and theoretical grounds. Consider a constant decrease in the value of money of, say, 10 percent a year. The individual would not reduce his real cash balances continually but only until the marginal benefit from a unit of real balances was equal to the (now expanded) cost of holding money. See Friedman, *The Optimum*, pp. 8-14.

36. See Mises' discussion of "panic prices" in *Theory of Money*, pp. 228-29.

37. Ibid., pp. 162-65.

38. Philip Cagen, "The Monetary Dynamics of Hyperinflation," in *Studies in the Quantity Theory of Money*, ed. M. Freidman (Chicago, 1958), pp. 25-117.

39. It is usual to credit Irving Fisher and not Mises with the "price anticipation effect"; see, for example, John T. Boorman and Thomas M. Havrilesky, *Money Supply, Money Demand, and Macroeconomic Models* (Boston: Allyn & Bacon, 1972), pp. 208-9. Certainly Fisher's *Purchasing Power of Money* and his *Rate of Interest* (New York: Macmillan Co., 1907) predated Mises' *Theory of Money*. It seems to me that Mises' discussion of price expectations and how they affect the decision to hold cash balances is sufficiently different from Fisher's discussion to warrant some academic recognition. Edmund Phelps credited Mises, rather than Fisher, in "Money Wage Dynamics and Labour Market Equilibrium," in *Microeconomic Foundations*, p. 129.

40. An important thesis of this paper is that Mises (like Wicksell) was an admirer of the quantity theory but critical of Fisher's mechanical version of that theory, which tends to ignore the role individual cash balances play in linking the commodity and money markets. On Mises as an adherent of the quantity theory, see *Theory of Money*, pp. 130, 146-54. On Wicksell as a supporter of the quantity theory, see Patinkin, *Money, Interest*, p. 587, for references to Wicksell's writings. I wish to emphasize that I am concerned here with Mises' monetary economics and their relationship to Wicksell's *early* monetary theories. Thus, I make no attempt to trace the evolution of Wicksell's own ideas or to discuss his debate with Mises, which occurred after the publication of the *Theory of Money and Credit*. Wicksell's later views on money are in his *Lectures on Political Economy* 2 (London: Routledge & Kegan Paul, 1935); see also Carl G. Uhr, *Economic Doctrines of Knut Wicksell* (Berkeley: University of California Press, 1960), pp. 198-327.

41. Wicksell, *Interest and Prices*, pp. 18-28.

42. Ibid. Mises dated the "proportionality theorem" to Hume and Mill (*Theory of Money*, pp. 139-40). The doctrine, however, can be located in the sixteenth-century writings of Jean Bodin and the Spanish Scholastics.

What disturbed Mises was that while the general theory of price had advanced beyond the naive notion that price is *proportional* to the ratio between demand and supply, monetary theory had not (cf. Mises, *Theory of Money*, pp. 128-30).

43. Ibid., pp. 141-42.

44. See Patinkin's distinction between an "individual demand curve for money" and a "market equilibrium" curve in *Money, Interest*, pp. 24-31.

45. Ibid., pp. 50-59.

46. Fisher, *Purchasing Power*, pp. 29-30.

47. Mises, *Theory of Money*, pp. 143-45.

48. Compare this treatment of the consequences of an increase in the quantity of money with the gold-discovery example offered by Mises in *Theory of Money*, pp. 137-45.

49. Cf. Mises' criticism of "price averages" in *Theory of Money*, pp. 188-94.

50. When prices start on an upward course, the first recipients of the new money may find that their real balances have fallen and that they must now resell some of the nonmonetary commodities that they originally purchased with the new money. If transactions costs are large enough, they may find that their final wealth position is lower than before they received the new money. Thus the rule that the *first* recipients of the new money are gainers need not necessarily be true. The reason governments gain by issuing new money is that they generally find themselves in a "debtor" position and the inflation reduces the real value of their liabilities (ibid., p. 139).

51. See Mises' discussion of "forced savings" in *Theory of Money*, pp. 346-52.

52. Mises credited Karl G. A. Knies *Geld und Kredit* (Berlin: Weidmann, 1876) and Fisher's *Rate of Interest* (New York: Macmillan Co., 1907) for explanations of the impact of price expectations on interest rates (*Theory of Money*, pp. 200, 454). In more recent literature the rise in interest rates during prolonged inflation is sometimes termed the "Gibson paradox." This phenomenon was correctly understood by Mises.

53. Patinkin wrote that "a doubling of the quantity of money can in general be expected to affect both equilibrium relative prices and the rate of interest. Specifically, the relative prices of those commodities favored by debtors will rise, while those favored by creditors will fall. Similarly, the (real) interest rate will rise or fall, depending on which of two countervailing forces is stronger: the decrease in the demand for bonds, caused by the worsened real position of creditors; or the decrease in the supply of bonds, caused by the improved real position of debtors" (*Money, Interest*, p. 74).

54. See, for example, Friedman, *The Optimum*, pp. 16-21.

55. See Don Patinkin, "Wicksell's Cumulative Process," *Economic Journal* 62 (1952): 835-47; reprinted in Patinkin, *Money, Interest,* pp. 588-97.

56. Mises, *Theory of Money,* pp. 355-57.

57. In the preface to the second German edition of the *Theory of Money* (see note 1 above), Mises explained that he was adopting Böhm-Bawerk's terminology because it was best known to his readers, but he stated that his own views on the determination of the (natural) rate of interest were now (i.e., 1924) different. His criticisms of Böhm-Bawerk finally appeared in *Nationalökonomie* (Geneva, Switzerland: Editions Union, 1940), pp. 439-44. An English translation of these passages was completed by Bettina Bien Greaves and Percy L. Greaves, Jr., in *Mises Made Easier: A Glossary for Ludwig von Mises' Human Action* (New York: Free Market Books, 1974), pp. 150-57. See also Ludwig von Mises, *Human Action: A Treatise on Economics* (Chicago: Henry Regnéry, 1966), p. 488n. For Mises' own "time preference" theory of interest, see ibid., pp. 479-90. It so happens, however, that Mises' particular explanation of why Wicksell's cumulative process must end was not affected by his subsequent position on the nature and determination of interest.

58. We have seen that Mises did not consider the possibility of a continuous and fully anticipated price inflation of, say, 10 percent accompanied by an equivalent increase in the quantity of money with all distribution effects eliminated by appropriate "index clauses" in all contracts. Mises believed that in such circumstances individuals would continually reduce their desired cash balances propelling the economic system toward hyperinflation (see note 35 above). However, the argument used here with regard to bank credit expansion is a bit more subtle. Apparently, the initial lowering of the money rate below the natural rate alters relative prices making the prices of higher-order goods (i.e., capital goods) rise relative to lower-order goods (i.e., consumer goods). As consumer goods prices rise (because of the introduction of new money into the economy), capital goods prices must rise faster to maintain the ratio dictated by the lower interest rate. But consumer prices in the next period will rise still faster, and the system is propelled toward hyperinflation, which is intensified by the reduction of (real) cash balances mentioned above. Mises developed the mechanisms sketched here in more detail in his 1928 monograph *Geldwertstabilisierung und Konjunkturpolitik.*

59. This process of readjustment is, of course, a business depression. Mises claimed as much (*Theory of Money,* pp. 365-66).

60. See esp. Friedrich A. Hayek's early writings, such as *Prices and Production* (London: George Routledge & Sons, 1935), pp. 148-52; and

Hayek, "Capital and Industrial Fluctuations," *Econometrica* 2 (April 1934): 152-67.

61. Mises, *Theory of Money*, pp. 435-57.

62. Ibid., pp. 138, 416-17; see also Mises, *Human Action*, pp. 471-76.

63. Though Wicksell did not include demand deposits in his definition of "money," he realized that an increase in deposits acts like money in raising prices. The purpose of his "cumulative process" discussion was to augment the quantity theory by describing the mechanism by which increases in bank reserves increase prices; cf. Patinkin, *Money, Interest*, p. 588. Mises was more "modern" than Wicksell because he defined "money" in a broader sense so as to include bank deposits (*Theory of Money*, pp. 278-96). See also translator's remarks, ibid., pp. 482-83.

64. Such an arrangement would not, according to Mises, encourage bank credit expansion but would actually retard it. Competition among the note-issuing banks would raise the reserve-deposit ratio. Any single group of banks found unable to meet their payments obligations would be declared "bankrupt" and their owners held libel under the usual arrangements of business law. Cf. Mises, *Human Action*, pp. 444-48.

Ludwig von Mises and The Theory of Capital and Interest

Israel M. Kirzner

Students of Misesian economics often agree that the theory of capital and interest occupies a central and characteristically Austrian position in the general Misesian system. That is the reason Frank H. Knight, in his lengthy and critical review article of the first complete exposition of that system,[1] chose to concentrate on "the theory of capital and interest" after deciding to confine his review to "some one main problem which at once is peculiarly central in the structure of theory, and on which [his] disagreement with the author reaches down to basic premises and methods."[2] In that article Knight identified Mises as the foremost exponent of the Austrian position on capital and interest. In a 1945 article Friedrich A. Hayek also alluded to Mises as the most thoroughgoing among the Austrians on these problems.[3]

And yet, in his published works, Mises appears to have devoted little attention to the theories of capital and interest until relatively late in his career. His influence on these matters was largely confined to his oral teaching and seminar discussions. As late as 1941 (presumably without having seen Mises' *Nationalökonomie*, published in 1940), Hayek remarked in his *Pure Theory of Capital* that, while Mises' "published work deals mainly with the more complex problems that only arise beyond the point at which [this book]

51

ends," Mises had nonetheless "suggested some of the angles from which the more abstract problem is approached [in this book]."[4]

Apart from a 1931 *Festschrift* paper on inconvertible capital,[5] Mises' published work on capital and interest prior to 1940 is confined (apart from casual *obiter dicta*) to a few brief pages in his *Socialism*.[6] On the other hand, there is an intriguing, somewhat cryptic footnote in the second (1924) edition of his *Theory of Money and Credit*.[7] It makes clear that since 1912 Mises (1) had given much critical thought to the theory of interest, (2) now considered Eugen von Böhm-Bawerk, while "the first to clear the way that leads to understanding of the problem," nonetheless to have presented a theory that was *not* satisfactory, and (3) hoped to publish "in the not-too-distant future" his own special study of the problem. It is certainly unfortunate that Mises never published such a study and that we are forced to rely on a relatively meager collection of scattered remarks in his larger works in order to understand what he considered unsatisfactory about Böhm-Bawerk's position. Fortunately, while his later works do not include a detailed critical discussion of Böhm-Bawerk's writings, they do provide us with a complete theoretical treatment of the problems of capital and interest, thereby justifying Knight's claim that the theory of capital and interest occupies a central position in the Misesian system. In what follows I shall first summarize Mises' own views on the problems of capital and interest and then discuss the extent to which his views differed from those of Böhm-Bawerk and Knight. In so doing we shall discover that Mises' later position is, as was noted by both Knight and Hayek, characteristically and consistently Austrian.

1. MISES ON CAPITAL AND ON INTEREST:

Mises' views on capital and on interest may be conveniently summarized as follows:

a. Interest is *not* the specific income derived from using capital goods;[8] nor is it "the price paid for the services of capital."[9] Instead, interest expresses the universal ("categorial") phenomenon of time preference and will therefore inevitably emerge also in a pure exchange economy without production.

b. Since production takes time, the market prices of factors of production (which tend to reflect the market prices of the consumer goods they produce) are themselves subject to considerations of time preference. Thus the market in a production economy generates interest as the excess *value* of produced goods over the appropriately discounted values of the relevant factors of production.

c. The concept of *capital* (as well as of its correlative *income*) is strictly a tool for economic calculation and hence has meaning only in the context of a market in which monetary calculation is meaningful. Thus, capital is properly defined as the (subjectively perceived) monetary value of the owner's equity in the assets of a particular business unit. *Capital* is therefore to be sharply distinguished from *capital goods*.

d. *Capital goods* are produced factors of production; they are "intermediary stations on the way leading from the very beginning of production to its final goal, the turning out of consumers' goods."[10]

e. It is decidedly *not* useful to define *capital* as the totality of capital goods. Nor does the concept of a *totality* of capital goods provide any insight into the productive process.

f. Capital goods are the results of earlier (i.e., higher) stages of production and therefore are not factors of production in their own right apart from the factors employed in their production. Capital goods have no productive power of their own that cannot be attributed to these earlier productive factors.

In his discussions about capital and interest, Mises did not, to any extent, name the specific authors with whom he took issue. As Knight observed (with respect to the entire volume that he was reviewing) Mises' exposition of capital and interest "is highly controversial in substance, and in tone, though the argument is directed toward positions, with very little debate or *Auseinandersetzung* with named authors."[11]

The hints that Mises himself gave, together with a careful comparison of Mises' own stated views with those of other capital theorists, enable us to understand how his views relate to the more widely known theories of capital and interest against which he was rebelling. Such an understanding is of the utmost importance in order to fully appreciate Mises' contribution. In the following analysis I shall indicate the points of disagreement between Mises and the two major contesting approaches of his time on the issue of capital and interest. I shall consider the Böhm-Bawerkian tradition first and then move on to review the [John Bates] Clark-Knight point of view.

2. MISES AND THE BÖHM-BAWERKIAN THEORY

We have already seen that, as early as 1924, Mises had indicated dissatisfaction with Böhm-Bawerk's theory. This may come as a surprise to those who—quite mistakenly—believe that the Austrian position on most questions of economic theory, and especially on the theory of capital and interest, is a monolithic one. The truth of the matter is that, while the suggestive brilliance of Böhm-Bawerk's contribution won international recognition as typifying the work of the Austrian school, it was by no means acceptable to other leading representatives of that school. It is by now well known, as reported by Joseph A. Schumpeter, that Carl Menger considered Böhm-Bawerk's theory of capital and interest to have been "one of the greatest errors ever committed."[12] Referring specifically not only to Menger but also to Friedrich von Wieser and Schumpeter himself, Hayek remarked that those "commonly regarded as the leaders of the 'Austrian School' of economics" did not accept Böhm-Bawerk's views.[13] So we should not be overly surprised at Mises' disagreement with his own mentor's teachings.

Mises' disagreements with the Böhm-Bawerkian theory reflect a consistent theme. Mises was concerned with distilling Böhm-Bawerk's basic ideas from the nonsubjective, technical, and empirical garb in which they had been presented. Mises tried to show that Böhm-Bawerk's basic ideas flowed smoothly out of his own praxeological approach, or, in other words, that they could be cast in a strictly subjectivist mold. Knight (correctly) characterized Mises as taking an extreme Austrian position on interest by refusing to attribute any explanatory role to the objective, or physical, conditions governing production in a capital-using world. As the Austrian theory of value depends on utility considerations, with no recognition accorded objective costs, so, too, Knight explained, the Misesian theory of interest depends entirely on subjective time preference, with no influence attributed to physical productivity.[14] One is reminded of Hayek's penetrating comment concerning the nature of Mises' contribution to economics. Remarking that "it is probably no exaggeration to say that every important advance in economic theory during the last hundred years was a further step in the consistent application of subjectivism,"[15] Hayek cited Mises as the economist who most consistently carried out this subjectivist development: "Probably all the characteristic features of his theories . . . follow directly . . . from this central position."[16] More specifically, Mises' theory of capital and interest is in disagreement with Böhm-Bawerk's on the following points:

a. On the role of time: Mises, while paying tribute to the "imperishable merits" of Böhm-Bawerk's seminal role in the development of the time-preference theory, sharply criticized the epistemological perspective from which Böhm-Bawerk viewed time as entering the analysis. For Böhm-Bawerk time preference is an empirical regularity observed through casual psychological observation. Instead, Mises saw time preference as a "definite categorial element . . . operative in every instance of action."[17] In Mises' view, Böhm-Bawerk's theory failed to do justice to the universality and inevitability of the phenomenon of time preference. In addition, Mises took Böhm-Bawerk to task for not recognizing that time should enter analysis only in the *ex ante* sense. The role that time "plays in action consists entirely in the choices acting man makes between periods of production of different length. The length of time expended in the past for the production of capital

goods available today does not count at all. . . .The 'average period
of production' is an empty concept.''[18] It may be remarked that
here Mises identified a source of perennial confusion concerning
the role of time in the Austrian theory. Many of the criticisms
leveled by Knight and others against the Austrian theory are
irrelevant when the theory is cast explicitly in terms of the time-
conscious, *forward-looking decisions* made by producers· and consumers.[19]

b. On the role of productivity: As already mentioned, Mises
sharply deplored the concessions Böhm-Bawerk made to the
productivity theorists. To Mises it was both unfortunate and inex-
plicable that Böhm-Bawerk, who in his critical history of interest
doctrines had "so brilliantly refuted" the productivity approach,
himself fell, to some extent, into the same kinds of error in his
Positive Theory. There is some disagreement in the literature on the
degree to which Böhm-Bawerk in fact allowed productivity considerations to enter his theory. The issue goes back at least to Frank
A. Fetter's remark in 1902 that it "has been a surprise to many
students of Böhm-Bawerk to find that he has presented a theory,
the most prominent feature of which is the technical productiveness
of roundabout processes. His criticism of the productivity theories
of interest has been of such a nature as to lead to the belief that he
utterly rejected them. . . .[But] it appears from Böhm-Bawerk's
later statement that he does not object to the productivity theory as
a partial, but as an exclusive, explanation of interest.''[20] Much later
Schumpeter insisted that productivity plays only a subsidiary role
in what is in fact wholly a time-preference theory.[21] It is of some interest to note that when Böhm-Bawerk considered the alternative
roles for productivity in a time-conscious theory, he came out
squarely for an interpretation that placed productivity and "im-
patience" on the same level.[22] Böhm-Bawerk made it very clear that
he was not willing to identify his position with that of Fetter, who
espoused a time-preference theory of interest without any mention
of productivity considerations. Böhm-Bawerk remarked that
"Fetter himself espouses a [theory which] places him on the outer-
most wing of the purely 'psychological' interest theorists—

'psychological' as opposed to 'technical.' He moves into a position far more extreme than the one I occupy. . . ."[23]

Certainly Mises offered a theory of interest fully as "extreme" as the one developed by Fetter. Later we shall consider Mises' denial that capital productivity has any role in interest theory.

c. On the definition of capital: Böhm-Bawerk defined capital as the aggregate of intermediate products (i.e., of produced means of production)[24] and in so doing was criticized by Menger.[25] Menger sought "to rehabilitate the abstract concept of capital as the money value of the property devoted to acquisitive purposes against the Smithian concept of the 'produced means of production.' "[26] As early as his work on *Socialism* (1923), Mises emphatically endorsed the Mengerian definition.[27] In *Human Action* he pursued the question even more thoroughly though without making it explicit that he was objecting to Böhm-Bawerk's definition. Economists, Mises maintained, fall into the error of defining capital as *real capital*—an aggregate of physical things. This is not only an "empty" concept but also one that has been responsible for serious errors in the various uses to which the concept of capital has been applied.

Mises' refusal to accept the notion of capital as an aggregate of produced means of production expressed his consistent Austrian emphasis on forward-looking decision making. Menger had already argued that "the historical origin of a commodity is irrelevant from an economic point of view."[28] (Later Knight and Hayek were to claim that emphasis on the historical origins of produced means of production is a residual of the older cost-of-production perspectives and inconsistent with the valuable insight that bygones are bygones.[29]) Thus, Mises' rejection of Böhm-Bawerk's definition reflects a throughgoing subjective point of view.

In addition, Mises' unhappiness with the Böhm-Bawerkian notion of capital is due to his characteristically Austrian scepticism toward economic aggregates. As Mises wrote, "[The] totality of the produced factors of production is merely an enumeration of physical quantities of thousands and thousands of various goods. Such an inventory is of no use to acting. It is a description of a part of the universe in terms of technology and topography and has no

reference whatever to the problems raised by the endeavors to improve human well-being."[30] Lachmann suggested that a similar
objection to the questionable practice of economic aggregation may
have been the reason for Menger's own sharp disagreement with
Böhm-Bawerk's theory.[31]

In place of the Böhm-Bawerkian notion of capital, Mises took
over Menger's definition of the term. Thus, in *Human Action,* Mises
emphasized at great length that the measurement of capital has
significance only for the role it plays in economic calculation. The
term denotes, therefore, an accounting concept and depends for its
measurement upon a system of market prices: Mises explained that
"the capital concept is operative as far as men in their actions let
themselves be guided by capital accounting."[32] At another place
Mises wrote: "Capital is the sum of the money equivalent of all
assets minus the sum of the money equivalent of all liabilities as
dedicated at a definite date to the conduct of the operations of a
definite business unit."[33] It follows, in Mises' words, that capital "is
inescapably linked with capitalism, the market economy. It is a
mere shadow in economic systems in which there is no market exchange and no money prices of goods of all orders."[34] We shall
return to several implications of Mises' substitution of the
Mengerian capital concept for Böhm-Bawerk's definition.

3. MISES AND THE CLARK-KNIGHT TRADITION

If Mises' writings on capital and interest diverge from Böhm-
Bawerk's theory, they certainly imply a total rejection of the principal alternative to that tradition, the approach developed in the
writings of both Clark and Knight. The Clark-Knight concept of
capital and the productivity theory of interest came under sharp attack in Mises' major (later) works. As we have mentioned, Knight's
review article of Mises' *Nationalökonomie* consisted almost entirely of
an attack on Mises' theory of capital and interest, coupled with a
restatement and clarification of his [Knight's] own position. By
enumerating Mises' various objections to the Clark-Knight view,

we acquire, at the same time, a more complete understanding of Mises' disagreement with Böhm-Bawerk. The reason is that the Knightian theory of interest is, as Knight proclaimed, completely opposed to the "absolute Austrianism" of Mises' approach. And what Mises found objectionable in Böhm-Bawerk's theory were, again, just those points in it which he saw as incompatible with a consistently Austrian perspective. So that it is entirely understandable why Mises' position with regard to Böhm-Bawerk's theory is clarified by his criticisms of Clark's and Knight's views. We may group Mises' objections to the Clark-Knight position as follows:

a. The Clark-Knight concept of capital: Mises had little patience with the notion of capital as a self-perpetuating fund, which he (and others) declared to be sheer mysticism.[35] "An existence," Mises wrote, "has been attributed to 'capital,' independent of the capital goods in which it is embodied. Capital, it is said, reproduces itself and thus provides for its own maintenance. . . .All this is nonsense."[36]

It is easy to see how foreign the motion of the "automatic maintenance of capital" must have appeared to Mises. An approach that concentrates analytical attention—as Austrian economics does—on the purposive and deliberate decisions of individual human beings when accounting for all social economic phenomena must treat the notion of capital as a spontaneously growing plant as not merely factually incorrect but simply absurd.[37] Moreover Mises sensed that such Knightian ideas can lead men to quite dangerous mistakes in public policy, when they ignore the institutional framework and incentive system needed to encourage those deliberate decisions necessary for maintaining the capital stock and enhancing its continued growth.[38]

The Misesian critique of the Clark-Knight view and his endorsement of the Mengerian capital concept suggest what Mises might have said about Hicks' recent classification of the views of economists concerning the aggregate of productive assets as being either "fundist" or "materialist."[39] Mises would have rejected a fundism that, by submerging the separate physical capital goods, ends up concentrating on some supposed quality apart from the goods themselves. He would have argued that the recognition of the time-conscious plans of producers does not require that we submerge the individualities of these goods into, say, a notion such as the average period of production. And, as we have seen, he rejected out of hand the Clarkian view—in Hicks' opinion a "materialist" view—that, by abstracting from the multiperiod plans needed to generate output with capital goods, sees these goods spontaneously generating perpetual flows of net income. In fact, Mises would argue, the entire fundist-materialist debate is predicated on the quite unfortunate practice of directing attention to the aggregate of physical goods. The only useful purpose for a capital concept consists strictly in its accounting role as a tool for economic calculation—a role enormously important for the efficient operation of a productive economy. It was, Mises would insist, Böhm-Bawerk's failure to see all this (and his willingness to accept the basis for a fundist-materialist debate) that lent credence to a Clark-Knight view of the real-capital concept, which implied the mythology of a kind of fundism ("perpetual capital") that Böhm-Bawerk himself did *not* accept. In rejecting Böhm-Bawerk's definition of capital in favor of the Mengerian definition, Mises rendered the Hicksian classification inapplicable to his own work.

b. Trees and fruit: Mises' adoption of Menger's concept of capital made it possible for him to avoid the pitfalls in interest theory that stem from the *capital-income* dichotomy. In everyday lay experience the ownership of capital provides assurance of a steady income. As soon as capital is identified as some aggregate of factors of production, it becomes tempting to ascribe the steady income that capital ownership makes possible as somehow expressing the *productivity* of these factors. This has always been the starting point for productivity theories of interest. Knight's permanent-fund-of-capital view of physical capital is simply a variant of those theories that view interest as net income generated perpetually by the productivity of the abstract capital temporarily embodied in particular lumps of physical capital. The capital stock, in this view, is a permanent tree that spontaneously and continuously produces fruit (interest).[10] Mises was explicit in concluding ·that this erroneous view of interest results from defining capital as an aggregate of produced factors of production. "The worst outgrowth of the use of the mythical notion of real capital was that economists began to speculate about a spurious problem called the productivity of (real) capital." It was such speculation, Mises made clear, that is responsible for the "blunder" of explaining "interest as an income derived from the productivity of capital."[41]

The Mengerian concept of capital as an accounting tool enables us to steer clear of such blunders. The accounting concept comes into play only as reflecting a particular motive that calculating human beings display: "The calculating mind of the actor draws a boundary line between the consumer's goods which he plans to employ for the immediate satisfaction of his wants and the goods .. . which he plans to employ for providing by further acting, for the satisfaction of future wants."[42] There is no implication whatsoever that the flow of income thus achieved for consumption purposes—through the careful deployment of capital—is the automatic fruit of the productivity of capital.

c. The structure of the productive process: Perhaps at the core of Mises' rejection of the Clark-Knight productivity theory of interest lies his wholehearted support of the Mengerian insight that the productive process consists of deploying goods of higher order toward the production of goods of lower order. "It is possible to think of the producers' goods as arranged in orders according to their proximity to the consumers' good for whose production they can be used. Those producers' goods which are the nearest to the production of a consumers' good are ranged in the second order, and accordingly those which are used for on the production of goods of the second order, in the third order and so on."[43] The purpose of such a scheme of classification is to demonstrate "how the valuation and the prices of the goods of higher orders are dependent on the valuation and the prices of the goods of lower orders produced by their expenditure."[44] This fundamental approach to the pricing of productive factors is able, Mises explained, to lay aside the reasoning of the productivity theorists. *The prices of capital goods must reflect the services expected from their future employment.*[45] In the absence of time preference the price of a piece of land (or of a capital good)—that is, the price in terms of consumer goods—would equal the undiscounted sum of the marginal values of the future services attributed to it. The productive capacity of a factor cannot (without time preference) account for a flow of interest income on its market value. The phenomenon of interest arises because, as a result of time preference, factor prices reflect only the *discounted* values of their services. "As production goes on, the factors of production are transformed or ripen into present goods of a higher value."[46] For Mises, the important economic characteristic of capital goods is not merely that they can be employed in future production, but that the relationship they bear to their future products is one of higher-order goods to goods of lower order. It is this factor that vitiates the productivity theory.

Knight's refusal to grant merit to this reasoning must be seen as a consequence of rejecting Menger's position that factors of production are really *higher-order* goods. "Perhaps the most serious defect in Menger's economic system . . . is his view of production as a process of converting goods of higher order into goods of lower order."[47] Because of Knightian view of the productive process emphasizes the reptitive "circular flow" of economic activity while denying the paramount importance of a *structural order* linked to final consumer demand, it is possible to simply ignore the Austrian critique of the productivity theory of interest. In essence, this is what Knight did.

4. *MISES, CAPITALISTS, AND ENTREPRENEURSHIP*

One final observation concerning Mises' theory of capital and interest is in order. At all times Mises stressed what he termed the "integration of catallactic functions" that takes place in the real world. Real-world capitalists, Mises constantly reminds us, must of necessity—like landowners, laborers, and consumers—be also *entrepreneurs.* "A capitalist [besides investing funds] is always also virtually an entrepreneur and speculator. He always runs the chance of losing his funds."[48] It follows that "interest stipulated and paid in loans includes not only originary interest but also entrepreneurial profit."[49]

In other words, entrepreneurship exists in capital-using production processes, not only in the usual sense that an entrepreneur-producer borrows or otherwise assembles capital as part of his entrepreneurial function, but also in the more subtle sense that the capitalists themselves, in lending their capital to entrepreneur-producers, are necessarily acting "entrepreneurially." While this does not prevent us from analytically isolating the pure capitalist and pure entrepreneurial functions, it does mean that in the real world originary interest and entrepreneurial profit are never found in isolation from one another.

NOTES

1. Ludwig von Mises, *Nationalökonomie: Theorie des Handelns und Wirtschaftens* (Geneva: Editions Union, 1940).

2. Frank H. Knight, "Professor Mises and the Theory of Capital," *Economica* 8 (November 1941): 410.

3. Friedrich A. Hayek, "Time-Preference and Productivity: A Reconsideration," *Economica* 12 (February 1945): 22.

4. Friedrich A. Hayek, *Pure Theory of Capital* (London: Routledge & Kegan Paul, 1941), p. 45.

5. Ludwig von Mises, "Das festangelegte Kapital," in *Economische Opstelen: Aangeboden aan Prof. Dr. C. A. Verrijn Stuart* (Haarlem: De Erven F. Bohn N. V., 1931), pp. 214-28; also in *Epistemological Problems of Economics,* trans. George Reisman (Princeton: D. Van Nostrand, 1960), pp. 217-310. For bibliographical information on Mises' works I am indebted to Bettina Bien [Greaves], *The Works of Ludwig von Mises* (Irvington-on-Hudson, N. Y.: Foundation for Economic Education, 1969).

6. Ludwig von Mises, *Socialism: An Economic and Sociological Analysis* (New Haven: Yale University Press, 1959), pp. 142-43.

7. Ludwig von Mises. *The Theory of Money and Credit* (New Haven: Yale University Press, 1959), p. 339, and esp. p. 24.

8. Ludwig von Mises, *Human Action: A Treatise on Economics* (Chicago: Henry Regnery, 1966), p. 524.

9. Ibid., p. 526.

10. Ibid., p. 493.

11. Knight, "Professor Mises," p. 409.

12. See Joseph A. Schumpeter, *History of Economic Analysis* (New York: Oxford University Press, 1954), p. 847. See also Erich Streissler and W. Weber, "The Menger Tradition," in *Carl Menger and the Austrian School of Economics*, ed. J. R. Hicks (Oxford: Clarendon Press, 1973), p. 231.

13. Hayek, *Pure Theory of Capital*, p. 46n. For Hayek's criticisms of Böhm-Bawerk's work, see ibid., pp. 414-23. A critique of Böhm-Bawerk by an "Austrian" theorist may be found in Ludwig M. Lachmann, *Capital and Its Structure* (London: London School of Economics and Political Science, 1956).

14. Knight, "Professor Mises," pp. 422.

15. Friedrich A. Hayek, *The Counter-Revolution of Science: Studies on the Abuse of Reason* (Glencoe, Ill.: Free Press, 1955), p. 31.

16. Ibid., p. 210, note 24.

17. Mises, *Human Action*, p. 488. See also Ludwig von Mises, *Epistemological Problems of Economics*, trans. George Reisman (Princeton: D. Van Nostrand, 1960), p. 31.

18. Mises, *Human Action*, pp. 488-89.

19. See Israel M. Kirzner, *An Essay on Capital* (New York: Augustus Kelly, 1966), pp. 79, 99.

20. Frank A. Fetter, "The 'Roundabout Process' in the Interest Theory," *Quarterly Journal of Economics* 17 (November 1902): 177.

21. Schumpeter, *History of Economic Analysis*, pp. 931-32.

22. Eugen von Böhm-Bawerk, *History and Critique of Interest Theories*, vol. 1, *Capital and Interest*, trans. George D. Huncke and Hans F. Sennholz (South Holland, Ill.: Libertarian Press, 1959), p. 482, note 112.

23. Ibid., p. 476, note 14.

24. Ibid., pp. 14, 32.

25. Carl Menger, "Zur Theorie des Kapitals," (Conrad's) *Jahrbucher fur Nationalökonomie und Statistik* (Jena: Gustav Fischer Verlag, 1888), 17:

26. Friedrich A. Hayek, "Carl Menger," in *Grundsätze der Volkswirtschaftslehre*, Scarce Tracts in Economic and Political Science (London: London School of Economics and Political Science, 1934), p. xxvi.

27. Mises, *Socialism*, pp. 123, 142.

28. Hayek, "Carl Menger," p. xxvi.

29. Hayek, *Pure Theory of Capital*, p. 89.

30. Mises, *Human Action*, p. 263.

31. More precisely Lachmann suggested that Menger was objecting to the notion of the homogenization of capital (Ludwig M. Lachmann, "Sir John Hicks as a Neo-Austrian," *South African Journal of Economics* 41 [September 1973]: 205).

32. Mises, *Human Action*, p. 515.

33. Ibid., p. 262.

34. Ludwig von Mises, *Human Action: A Treatise on Economics*, 2d ed. rev. (New Haven: Yale University Press, 1963), p. 515. [In the 1966 edition the second line of this quotation is omitted.—Ed.]

35. For a listing of writers who have ascribed "mysticism" or "mythology" to the Clark-Knight concept of capital, see Kirzner, *An Essay on Capital*, p. 59.

36. Mises, *Human Action*, p. 515.

37. As Knight did in his well-known "Crusonia Plant" example (Frank H. Knight, "Diminishing Returns from Investment," *Journal of Political Economy* 52 [March 1944]: 29).

38. Mises, *Human Action*, p. 844.

39. See John R. Hicks, "Capital Controversies: Ancient and Modern," *American Economic Review* 64 (May 1974): 308-10. According to Hicks, "fundists" are those who see capital as something apart from the physical goods of which it happens to consist at a particular time. The "materialists" are those who refuse to see capital in any sense other than the physical goods that make it up. Hicks' terminology here is quite unfortunate and may lead to a misunderstanding of his own thesis. From what has been said in the text, it would seem that Clark and Knight are what Hicks meant when he spoke of "fundists." It turns out, however, that Hicks classified them as "materialists"! The Austrian school (which is vehemently opposed to the Clark-Knight notion of capital as a self-perpetuating fund) turns out, in Hick's classification, to be "fundist" because it viewed the stock of capital goods in terms of the multiperiod future plans in which they enter. The Clark-Knight notion of capital as a fund is therefore quite different from the Austrian notion of a fund. Clearly, in the Clark-Knight view, capital goods are not the representatives of *plans* for future production processes but rather permanent sources of automatic income flow.

40. See note 37 above.

41. Mises, *Human Action*, p. 263.

42. Ibid., p. 260.

43. Ibid., p. 94.

44. Ibid.

45. Ibid., p. 263-64.

46. Ibid., p. 525.

47. Frank H. Knight, "Introduction," in Carl Menger, *Principles of Economics*, trans. James Dingwall and Bert F. Hoselitz (Glencoe, Ill.: Free Press, 1950), p. 25.

48. Mises, *Human Action*, p. 253.

49. Ibid., p. 536.

Ludwig von Mises and Economic Calculation Under Socialism

Murray N. Rothbard

What might be called the "orthodox," or textbook, version of the famous economic calculation debate under socialism goes somewhat as follows:

Ludwig von Mises first raised the question of Socialist economic calculation in 1920 by asserting that socialism could not calculate economically because of the absence of a price system for the factors of production. Enrico Barone "then" showed (the fact that he had done so twelve years earlier is laid to accidents of timing and translation) that this was not a theoretical problem because all the equations existed for a solution. F. A. Hayek then retreated to a second line of attack by conceding the "theoretical" solution to economic calculation in a Socialist state but challenging its "practical" possibility. Finally, Oskar Lange, Abba Lerner, and others "demonstrated" the practical solution by advancing the concept of "market" socialism, in which the Planning Board arrives at market clearing prices through trial and error. Q. E. D. and Socialist planning has been salvaged, replete with Lange's ironic tribute to Mises for raising the problem for Lange and other Socialists to solve. If the actual record of Communist economies is brought into the discussion at all, it is usually done as a vindication of the Lange-Lerner thesis in practice.

That there are numerous holes in this neat and triumphal saga should be immediately clear. One example is that the "market socialism" in Yugoslavia and, less so, in the other East European countries has nothing to do with the alleged Lange-Lerner "market"; for while firms in Yugoslavia engage in genuine exchanges and therefore in a genuine price system, the Lange-Lerner Planning Boards were to be central planners who manipulated prices as a pure accounting device and in no sense allowed "markets" at all. Another example is that Barone, in the course of his alleged "theoretical" solution to the problem of Socialist calculation, himself ridiculed the idea that planning by means of his equations was in any sense workable, especially when we consider the continuing economic variability of the technical coefficients involved.[1]

But a particularly important flaw in the orthodox story is, as Hayek tried to make clear during the debate, the curious disjunction between the "theoretical" and the "practical." It is not simply that Barone and his mentor Pareto scoffed at the workability of the theoretical equations under Socialist planning. More important is the point that Mises and Hayek were implicitly attacking the relevance of the entire concept of Walrasian general equilibrium from which these equations flowed. For Mises and Hayek there was no disjunction between the "theoretical" and the "practical"; following the Austrian tradition, a theory that necessarily violated practical reality was an unsound theory. The fact that in a changeless world of perfect knowledge and general equilibrium a Socialist Planning Board could "solve" equations of prices and production was for Mises a worse than useless demonstration. Clearly, as Hayek would later develop at length, if complete knowledge of economic reality is assumed to be "given" to all, including a Planning Board, there is no problem of calculation or, indeed, any economic problem at all, whatever the economic system. The Mises demonstration of the impossibility of economic calculation under socialism and of the superiority of private markets in the means of production applied only to the real world of uncertainty, continuing change, and scattered knowledge.

In his monumental *Human Action,* the 1949 treatise that contained his final rebuttal to his Socialist critics, Mises emphasized the sterility of the mathematical approach:

The mathematical economists . . . formulate equations and draw curves which are supposed to describe reality. In fact they describe only a hypothetical and unrealizable state of affairs, in no way similar to the catallactic problems in question. They substitute algebraic symbols for the determinate terms of money as used in economic calculation and believe that this procedure renders their reasoning more scientific. . . .

In the imaginary construction of the evenly rotating economy all factors of production are employed in such a way that each of them renders the most valuable service. . . .It is, of course, possible to describe this imaginary state of the allocation of resources in differential equations and to visualize it graphically in curves. But such devices do not assert anything about the market process. They merely mark out an imaginary situation in which the market process would cease to operate. . . .

Both the logical and the mathematical economists assert that human action ultimately aims at the establishment of such a state of equilibrium and would reach it if all further changes in data were to cease. But the logical economist knows much more than that. He shows how the activities of enterprising men, the promoters and speculators, eager to profit from discrepancies in the price structure, tend toward eradicating such discrepancies and thereby also toward blotting out the sources of entrepreneurial profit and loss. . . .The mathematical description of various states of equilibrium is mere play. The problem is the analysis of the market process. . . .

The problems of process analysis, i.e., the only economic problems that matter, defy any mathematical approach.[2]

In developing this approach, Hayek engaged in a searching critique of Schumpeter's assertion that socialism suffers from no problem of economic calculation, because, to quote Schumpeter, the "consumers, in evaluating ('demanding') consumers' goods *ipso facto* also evaluate the means of production. . . ."[3] Hayek pointed out, however, that this easy step would only follow "to a mind to which all these facts were simultaneously known. . . .The practical problem, however, arises precisely because these facts are never so given to a single mind . . . instead, we must show how a solution is produced by the interactions of people each of whom possesses only partial knowledge." Hayek concluded that "any approach, such as that of much of mathematical economics with its simultaneous equations, which in effect starts from the assumption that people's *knowledge* corresponds with objective *facts* of the situation, systematically leaves out what is our main task to explain."[4]

Proceeding to an explicit refutation of the Lange-Lerner approach, Mises in *Human Action* scoffed at the idea that the Socialist managers will be instructed to "play market as children play war, railroad, or school." Specifically, the Socialists leave out the crucial function of shareholding, capital allocation, and entrepreneurship in their concentration on the purely managerial role:

The cardinal fallacy implied in this and all kindred proposals is that they look at the economic problem from the perspective of the subaltern clerk whose intellectual horizon does not extend beyond subordinate tasks. They consider the structure of industrial production and the allocation of capital to the various branches and production aggregates as rigid, and do not take into account the necessity of altering this structure in order to adjust it to changes in conditions. What they have in mind is a world in which no further changes occur and economic history has reached its final stage. They fail to realize that the operations . . . of the managers, their buying and selling, are only a small segment of the totality of market operations. The market of the capitalist society also performs all those operations which allocate the capital goods to the various branches of industry. The entrepreneurs and capitalists establish corporations and other firms, enlarge or reduce their size, dissolve them or merge them with other enterprises; they buy and sell the shares and bonds of already existing and of new corporations; they grant, withdraw, and recover credits; in short they perform all those acts the totality of which is called the capital and money market. It is these financial transactions of promoters and speculators that direct production into those channels in which it satisfies the most urgent wants of the consumers in the best possible way. . . .

The role that the loyal corporation manager plays in the conduct of business is . . . only a managerial function, a subsidiary assistance granted to the entrepreneurs and capitalists. . . .It can never become a substitute for the entrepreneurial function. The speculators, promoters, investors and moneylenders, in determining the structure of the stock and commodity exchanges and of the money market, circumscribe the orbit within which definite minor tasks can be entrusted to the manager's discretion. . . .

The capitalist system is not a managerial system; it is an entrepreneurial system. . . .Nobody has ever suggested that the socialist commonwealth could invite the promoters and speculators to continue their speculations and then deliver their profits to the common chest. Those suggesting a quasi-market for the socialist system have never wanted to preserve the stock and commodity exchanges, the trading in futures, and the bankers and money-lenders. . . .One cannot *play* speculation and investment. The speculators and investors expose their own wealth, their own destiny. This fact makes them responsible to the consumers. . . .If one relieves them of this responsibility, one deprives them of their very character.[5]

Mises also refuted the idea that a Socialist Planning Board would arrive at correct pricing through trial and error, through clearing the market. While this could be done for already produced consumer goods, for which a market would presumably continue to exist, it would be precisely impossible in the realm of capital goods, where there would be no genuine market; hence, any sort of rational decisions on the kinds and amounts of the production of capital and of consumer goods could not be made. In short, the process of trial and error works on the market because the emergence of profit and loss conveys vital signals to the entrepreneur, whereas such apprehensions of genuine profit and loss could not be made in the absence of a real market for the factors of production.

A common attempt to rebut Mises has been the simple empirical pointing to the existence of central planning in the Soviet Union and the other Communist states. But, in the first place, this argument is a two-edged sword, (1) because of the blatant failures of early War Communism in its abolition of the market, and (2) because the evident failures and breakdowns of central planning have led the Communist countries in East Europe, especially in Yugoslavia, to move rapidly away from socialism toward a genuine, and not a Lange-Lerner type of pseudo, market economy. But, more importantly, Mises pointed out that the Soviet Union and the other Socialist countries are not fully Socialist, since they still operate within a world market environment and are at least roughly able to use world capital and commodity prices on which to base their economic calculations.[6] That Communist planners base their calculations on world market prices is now generally acknowledged and is illustrated by an amusing encounter of Professor Peter Wiles with Polish Communist planners:

What actually happens is that 'world prices', *i.e. capitalist world prices,* are used in all intra- block trade. They are translated into rubles . . . and entered in bilateral clearing accounts. To the question, 'What would you do if there were no capitalist world?' came only the answer 'We'll cross that bridge when we come to it.' In the case of electricity the bridge is already under their feet: there has been great difficulty in pricing it since there is no world market.[7]

Mises' followers in the debate have continued to develop his basic critique of the impossibility of economic calculation under socialism. Thus, the attempted Lange-Lerner criterion of pricing in accordance with "marginal cost" has been attacked on what are essentially Austrian grounds, namely, that costs are not "given" and objective but are subjective estimates by various individuals of future selling prices and other economic conditions. Thus Hayek wrote that

excessive preoccupation with the conditions of a hypothetical state of stationary equilibrium has led modern economics . . . to attribute to the notion of costs in general a much greater precision and definiteness than can be attached to any cost phenomenon in real life. . . .[A]s soon as we leave the realm of . . . a stationary state and consider a world where most of the existing means of production are the product of particular processes that will probably never be repeated; where, in consequence of incessant change, the value of most of the more durable instruments of production has little or no connection with the costs which have been incurred in their production but depends only on the services which they are expected to render in the future, the question of what exactly are the costs of production of a given product is a question of extreme difficulty which cannot be answered . . . without first making some assumption as regards the prices of the products in the manufacture of which the same instruments will be used. Much of what is usually termed cost of production is not really a cost element that is given independently of the price of the product but a quasi-rent, or a depreciation quota which has to be allowed on the capitalized value of expected quasi-rents, and is therefore dependent on the prices which are expected to prevail.[8]

At another place, Hayek added that Lange and others "speak about 'marginal costs' as if they were independent of the period for which the manager can plan. Clearly, actual costs depend in many instances, as much as on anything, on buying at the right time. In no sense can costs during any period be said to depend solely on prices during that period. They depend as much on whether these prices have been correctly foreseen as on the views that are held about future prices."[9] And Paul Craig Roberts, while writing generally from a different perspective, pointed out that "under real-world conditions characterized by the passage of time, the marginal rule gives no clear guidance to those directed to organize production in accordance with it. Introducing the element of time brings in uncertainty and requires the exercise of *judgment*. Neither uncertainty nor judgment is present in the formulation of perfect competition from which Lange took his idea of the marginal rule."[10] Moreover, the outstanding critique of the marginal cost as well as of other authoritarian rules imposed on the entrepreneur was by G. F. Thirlby, who pointed out that costs are wrapped up inextricably in subjective estimates by the individual capitalists and entrepreneurs of alternative choices that are forgone, and since these alternatives are usually never undertaken, they can never be "objectively" determined by outside observers.[11]

The subjectivist Austrian critique of the modern concept of costs and its relevance to the question of Socialist calculation were neatly summed up by Professor Buchanan:

Confusion arises . . . when the properties of equilibrium, as defined for markets, are transferred as criteria of optimization in *nonmarket* or political settings. It is here that the critical distinction between the equilibrium of the single decision-maker and that attained through market interaction, the distinction stressed by Hayek, is absolutely essential. . . .The theory of social interaction, of the mutual adjustment among the plans of separate human beings, is different in kind from the theory of planning, the maximization of some objective function by a conceptualized omniscient being. The latter is equivalent, in all respects, to the problems faced by Crusoe or by any individual decision-maker. But this is not the theory of markets, and it is artificial and basically false thinking that makes it out to be. . . .Shadow prices are not market prices, and the opportunity costs that inform market decisions are not those that inform the choices of even the omniscient planner. These appear to be identical only because of the false objectification of the magnitudes in question. . . .

Simply considered, cost is the obstacle or barrier to choice, that which must be got over before choice is made. Cost is the underside of the coin, so to speak, cost is the displaced alternative, the rejected opportunity. Cost is that which the decision-maker sacrifices or gives up when he selects one alternative rather than another. Cost consists therefore in his own evaluation of the enjoyment or utility that he anticipates having to forego as a result of choice itself. There are specific implications to be drawn from this choice-bound definition of opportunity cost:

1. Cost must be borne exclusively by the person who makes decisions; it is not possible for this cost to be shifted to or imposed on others.

2. Cost is subjective; it exists only in the mind of the decision-maker or chooser.

3. Cost is based on anticipations; it is necessarily a forward-looking or *ex ante* concept.

4. Cost can never be realized because of the fact that choice is made; the alternative which is rejected can never itself be enjoyed.

5. Cost cannot be measured by someone other than the chooser since there is no way that subjective mental experience can be directly observed. . . .

In any general theory of choice cost must be reckoned in a *utility* rather than in a *commodity* dimension. From this it follows that the opportunity cost involved in choice cannot be observed and objectified and, more importantly, it cannot be measured in such a way as to allow comparisons over wholly different choice settings. The cost faced by the utility-maximizing owner of a firm, the value that he anticipates having to forego in choosing to produce an increment to current output, is not the cost faced by the utility-maximizing bureaucrat who manages a publicly owned firm, even if the physical aspects of the two firms are in all respects identical.[12]

There is one vital but neglected area where the Mises analysis of economic calculation needs to be expanded. For in a profound sense, the theory is not about socialism at all! Instead, it applies to *any* situation where one group has acquired control of the means of production over a large area—or, in a strict sense, throughout the world. On this particular aspect of socialism, it doesn't matter whether this unitary control has come about through the coercive expropriation brought about by socialism or by voluntary processes on the free market. For what the Mises theory focuses on is not simply the numerous inefficiencies of the political as compared to the profit-making market process, but the fact that a market for capital goods has disappeared. This means that, just as Socialist central planning could not calculate economically, no One Big Firm could own or control the entire economy. The Mises analysis applies to any situation where a market for capital goods has disappeared in a complex industrial economy, whether because of socialism or because of a giant merger into One Big Firm or One Big Cartel.

If this extension is correct, then the Mises analysis also supplies us the answer to the age-old criticism leveled at the unhampered, unregulated free-market economy: *what if* all firms banded together into one big firm that would exercise a monopoly over the economy equivalent to socialism? The answer would be that such a firm could not calculate because of the absence of a market, and therefore that it would suffer grave losses and dislocations. Hence, while a Socialist Planning Board need not worry about losses that would be made up by the taxpayer, One Big Firm would soon find itself suffering severe losses and would therefore disintegrate under this pressure. We might extend this analysis even further. For it seems to follow that, as we *approach* One Big Firm on the market, as mergers begin to eliminate capital goods markets in industry after industry, these calculation problems will begin to appear, albeit not as catastrophically as under full monopoly. In the same way the Soviet Union suffers calculation problems, albeit not so severe as would be the case were the entire world to be absorbed into the Soviet Union with the disappearance of the world market. If, then, calculation problems begin to arise as markets disappear, this places a free-market limit, not simply on One Big Firm, but even on partial monopolies that eradicate markets. Hence, the free market contains within itself a built-in mechanism limiting the relative size of firms in order to preserve markets throughout the economy. This point also serves to extend the notable analysis of Professor Coase on the market determinants of the size of the firm, or of the relative extent of corporate planning within the firm as against the use of exchange and the price mechanism. Coase pointed out that there are diminishing benefits and increasing costs to each of these two alternatives, resulting, as he put it, in an " 'optimum' amount of planning" in the free market system.[13] Our thesis adds that the costs of internal corporate planning become prohibitive as soon as markets for capital goods begin to disappear, so that the free-market optimum will always stop well short not only of One Big Firm throughout the world market but also of *any* disappearance of specific markets and hence of economic calculation in that product or resource. Coase stated that the important difference between planning under socialism and within business firms on the free market is that the former "is imposed on industry while firms arise voluntarily beasuse they represent a more efficient method of organizing production."[14] If our view is correct, then, this optimal free-market degree of planning also contains within itself a built-in safeguard against eliminating markets, which are so vital to economic calculation.

In fact, we may turn the question around to ask the Socialists: if, indeed, central planning is more efficient than, or even equally efficient to, the free-market economy, then why has central planning never come about through the creation of One Big Firm by the voluntary market process? The fact that One Big Firm has never arisen on the market and that it needs the coercive might of the State to establish such central planning under socialism demonstrates that the latter could not be the most efficient method of organizing the economy.[15]

In our expanded form, then, not only is Mises' insight into the irrationality of socialism in an industrial economy confirmed but so also is the self-subsistence and continuing optimality and rationality of the free-market economy.

NOTES

1. See Enrico Barone, "The Ministry of Production in the Collectivist State," in *Collectivist Economic Planning,* ed. Friedrich A. Hayek (London: George Routledge & Sons, 1935), p. 286. See also Trygve J. B. Hoff, *Economic Calculation in the Socialist Society* (London: William Hodge & Co., 1949), pp. 140-43.

2. Ludwig von Mises, *Human Action* (Chicago: Henry Regnery, 1966), pp. 353-56.

3. Joseph A. Schumpeter, *Capitalism, Socialism, and Democracy* (New York: Harper & Bros., 1942), p. 175.

4. Friedrich A. Hayek, *Individualism and Economic Order* (Chicago: University of Chicago Press, 1948), pp. 90-91.

5. Mises, *Human Action,* pp. 707-9. See also Dominic T. Armentano, "Resource Allocation Problems under Socialism," in *Theory of Economic Systems,* ed. W. P. Snavely (Columbus, Ohio: Charles E. Merrill Co., 1969), pp. 127-39. On the importance of the stock market in the free-market economy, see Ludwig M. Lachmann, *Capital and Its Structure* (London: London School of Economics and Political Science, 1956), pp. 67-71.

6. On Socialist countries operating within a world market environment, see Mises, *Human Action,* pp. 698-99. On the rapid breakdown of War Communism, see Boris Brutzkus, *Economic Planning in Soviet Russia* (London: George Routledge & Sons, 1935); and Paul Craig Roberts, *Alienation and the Soviet Economy* (Albuquerque, N.M.: University of New Mexico Press, 1971), pp. 20-47.

7. P. J. D. Wiles, "Changing Economic Thought in Poland," *Oxford Economic Papers* 9 (June 1957): 202-3.

8. Friedrich A. Hayek, "The Present State of the Debate," in *Collectivist Economic Planning,* pp. 226-27.

9. Hayek, *Individualism and Economic Order,* p. 198.

10. Roberts, *Alienation and the Soviet Economy,* p. 97.

11. G. F. Thirlby, "The Ruler" in *L.S.E. Essays on Cost,* ed. J. M. Buchanan and G. F. Thirlby (London: London School of Economics and Political Science, 1973), pp. 163-200.

12. James M. Buchanan, "Introduction: L.S.E. Cost Theory in Retrospect," in *L.S.E. Essays on Cost,* pp. 4-5, 14-15.

13. Ronald H. Coase, "The Nature of the Firm", *Economica* 4 (November 1937): 384-405; reprinted in American Economic Association, *Readings in Price Theory* (Homewood, Ill.: Richard D. Irwin, 1952), p. 335n.

14. Ibid.

15. See Murray N. Rothbard, *Man, Economy, and State* (Los Angeles: Nash Publishing Co., 1970), 2: 547-50, 585.

Ludwig von Mises and
the Justification of
the Liberal Order

William Baumgarth

Western political philosophy is (with few exceptions) the political philosophy of republicans. Out of this rich liberal tradition comes the vocabulary used in popular discussions about politics. By "popular" I mean not only the particular words that the ordinary citizen uses in political discussion but the ideas as well. The vocabulary of the common man is thoroughly democratic because it refers to the ideals and aspirations of democracy. It must be stressed at the outset, however, that this democratic flavoring of the vocabulary of politics has itself undergone modification over its long history. Thus, contemporary liberal democracy is classical democracy transformed, or, as some scholars might say, contemporary liberal democracy is classical democracy tailored to the necessities of an expanded commercial society.

Classical democracy, as described by Aristotle and other Greek thinkers, is the unmediated rule of the many, which means in fact the rule of the poor. They described a situation modeled after the ancient Greek city-state and considered the geographical limitations of the historical *polis* to be ideal for a political community. These small populations of several thousand not only provided the individual citizen with first-hand lessons in political decision making but offered him the opportunity to become intimately acquainted with the character of the other members of the *polis*. The compactness of the *polis* promoted the noncognitive dimensions of social life, such as affection and devotion to the public order. Virtues like these are more easily acquired where territorial size and population density closely resemble an extended family relationship than where community life is completely impersonalized as it is throughout the vast territories of the modern nation-state. Whatever the attitude of classical thinkers toward more expanded forms of political life (as would exist outside the Greek city), this much is clear: The conditions of ancient Greek political life simply do not lend themselves to the degree of social cooperation and economic specialization necessary for the establishment of a technology designed to eradicate the *material* obstacles to human happiness. The liberation of man's material desires from the moral confines of the Greek state involved, first, a liberation of the human mind from the prejudices of prescientific thinking. This transformation was the essence of the eighteenth-century historical phenomenon known as the "Enlightenment," during which rationality replaced metaphysical speculation and a sense of social progress replaced the cyclical and static thought of classical and medieval philosophers. The notion of progress in the eighteenth century was a materialistic concept, quite different from the ascetic claims of aristocratic virtue and "other-worldly" ideals of classical philosophers.

Modern-day liberalism is the political embodiment of the Enlightenment; for example, the liberalism of the Founding Fathers explicitly incorporates its philosophical attitudes. Early American political philosophy, as developed in the *Federalist Papers*, consists of a blend of various Enlightenment themes, clarified and reordered by the practical experiences of American political life. The primary motivations of the passions and of self-interest in social life gave rise to a new science of politics, which concluded that the regime best suited for human progress, material and spiritual, is the commercial democratic republic. Limited government became the explicit political goal of the classical liberals, because the limiting of government simultaneously frees economic transactions in the social sphere. Freeing economic exchange from, say, the shackles imposed by mercantilist forms of monopoly provides society with a social cohesiveness brought about by the mutual interdependence of economic agents in an ever-widening complexion of the division of labor.

The political thought of Ludwig von Mises provided a forceful restatement and elaboration of liberalism as applied to a modern commercial society. Mises' thought was developed during the first half of this century when liberalism, as a recognizable political force, was on the decline. This decline was precipitated by the theft of liberalism's aims by those who sought to achieve the ends by employing antiliberal methods. It is paradoxical that as liberalism's goal of material prosperity gained world acceptance, its specific program was threatened with complete extinction. Mises explained that the controversies of the modern world are about means and not ends: in general, men the world over expect a social system to provide "peace and abundance."[1] What men expect from social cooperation is the satisfaction of as many of their most urgent wants as possible, and therefore they, for the most part, dispute about the type of social system that will serve this purpose. In Mises' words, "Liberalism is distinguished from socialism, which likewise professes to strive for the good of all, not by the goal at which it aims, but by the means that it chooses to attain that goal."[2]

According to Mises, the primary problem faced by the West is that of rediscovering the meaning of its basic political philosophy. The meaning of liberalism as a political program is obscured because its language has been usurped by parties and movements that wish to substitute an entirely different program for that of limited government and unregulated commercial exchange. It is difficult to understand what "liberalism is and what it aims at" because.

one cannot simply turn to history for the information and inquire what the liberal politicians stood for and what they accomplished. For liberalism nowhere succeeded in carrying out its program as it intended. Nor can the programs and actions of those parties that today call themselves liberal provide us with any enlightenment concerning the nature of true liberalism. It has already been mentioned that even in England what is understood as liberalism bears a greater resemblance to Toryism and Socialism than to the old program of the freetraders.[3]

Despite the formidable obstacles that stand in the way, the liberal program must gain universal acceptance if the political goal of promoting individual welfare is to be realized. The reason, as Mises demonstrated by way of his economic writings, is that the Socialist path toward this goal is completely unworkable.

Clarifying the liberal program is difficult because the teachings of the eighteenth- and nineteenth-century founders of liberal thought are not adequate to meet the challenges of the modern world. As Mises wrote:

Liberalism is not a completed doctrine or a fixed dogma. On the contrary: it is the application of the teachings of science to the social life of man. And just as economics, sociology, and philosophy have not stood still since the days of David Hume, Adam Smith, David Ricardo, Jeremy Bentham, and Wilhelm Humboldt, so the doctrine of liberalism is different today from what it was in their day, even though its fundamental principles have remained unchanged.[4]

The early liberal theorists incorrectly anticipated how their doctrines were going to be received by the masses. Classical liberals, as exemplified by Condorcet, believed that mankind was already on the road toward human perfection and that liberal doctrine would triumph. They thought that the laws of social progress, which they had discovered by means of reason, would be immediately comprehended by the ordinary citizen, and that social cooperation based on these laws would inevitably lead to ever-widening interdependence among the members of the human species. Their most serious mistake, according to Mises, was in believing that the masses possess the ability and/or the patience to reason.[5] They also forgot that—as Rousseau clearly understood—the particular will, directed toward momentary self-advantage, can eclipse the drive toward the long-run general advantage. According to Mises, any attempt to foster popular understanding by vulgarizing social theory is a futile task. One can well appreciate the difficulties modern economists face when trying to, say, inform the public about wage and price controls, given the level of abstract reasoning involved. The short attention span of the public and the dry formulas of the economist combine to discredit reasoned programs and encourage the success of "short-run advantage" schemes promulgated by special-interest groups. Mises described this problem in the following passage:

The political ideology of liberalism was derived from a fundamental system of ideas that had first been developed as a scientific theory without any thought of its political significance. In contradistinction to this, the special rights and privileges sought by the antiliberal parties were, from the very outset, already realized in existing social institutions, and it was in justification of the latter that one undertook subsequently to elaborate an ideology, a task that was generally treated as a matter of little moment that could easily be disposed of with a few brief words. Farm groups think it sufficient to point out the indispensability of agriculture. The trade unions appeal to the indispensability of labor. The parties of the middle class cite the importance of the existence of a social stratum that represents the golden mean. It seems to trouble them little that such appeals contribute nothing to proving the necessity or even the advantageousness to the general public of the special privileges they are striving for. The groups that they desire to win over will follow them in any case, and as for the others, every attempt at recruiting supporters from their ranks would be futile.[6]

Thus, when liberalism is presented to a world that has been bred on special interest politics, it appears to be the product of still another interest group, but to "point out the advantages which everybody derived from the working of capitalism is not tantamount to defending the vested interests of the capitalists."[7] Liberalism is rooted in the idea of social *harmony:*

[It] has demonstrated that the antagonism of interests, which, according to a widely prevalent opinion, is supposed to exist among different persons, groups, and strata within a society based on private ownership of the means of production, does not, in fact, occur. Any increase in total capital raises the income of capitalists and landowners absolutely and that of

workers both absolutely and relatively. As regards their income, any shifts
in the various interests of the different groups and strata of society—the
entrepreneurs, capitalists, landowners, and workers—occur together and
move in the same direction as they pass through different phases in their
fluctuations; what varies is only the ratio of their shares of the social
product. The interests of the landowners oppose those of the members of
the other groups only in the one case of a genuine monopoly of a certain
mineral. The interests of the entrepreneurs can never diverge from those of
the consumers. The entrepreneur prospers the better, the better he is able
to anticipate the desires of the consumers.[8]

In contrast to liberalism, the ideology of special-interest politics is
predicated on the notion that an irreconcilable conflict of interests
exists and can be ended only by the victory of one social class over
another in class warfare. But the theory of class warfare suffers
from an internal contradiction: the admission that there is a harmony of interests *within* a class raises the possibility that such a harmony may exist among mankind. Mises wrote:

All the arguments that could be employed to prove the existence of a
solidarity of interests among the members of any of these groups prove
much more besides, *viz.*, the universal solidarity of interests within
ecumenical society. How these apparent conflicts of interest that seem at
first sight to be irreconcilable are in fact resolved can be shown only by
means of a line of reasoning that treats all mankind as an essentially har-
monious community and allows no room for the demonstration of any
irreconcilable antagonisms among nations, classes, races, and the like.[9]

Mises does not seem to believe that a clear enumeration of the
logical errors of special-interest politics can ever be sufficient to
convert the masses and intellectuals to the liberal doctrine of a
long-run harmony of interests. The reason is that the opposition to
liberalism has a psychological rather than a rational foundation.
The nature of the opposition to liberalism is treated at great length
in Mises' *Anti-Capitalistic Mentality*.[10] As it turns out, resentment
and envious malice are not the primary threats to the liberal
program. If they were, it would not be "too difficult to make clear
to a person who is filled with this sort of resentment that the important thing for him cannot be to worsen the position of his better

situated fellow men, but to improve his own."[11] Such an improvement depends upon increasing his own productivity, and the means of doing so are described in a systematic fashion by the science of economics. But the antiliberal mentality is, according to Mises, impervious to this (i.e., the economic) argument because such a mentality is rooted in neurosis. Rather than admit that his own life has been a failure, the enemy of capitalism adopts a "saving lie," that is, success would be his if only the capitalist order were to be abolished. Mises described the function of the "saving lie" as follows:

In the life of the neurotic the "saving lie" has a double function. It not only consoles him for past failure, but holds out the prospect of future success. In the case of social failure, which alone concerns us here, the consolation consists in the belief that one's inability to attain the lofty goals to which one has aspired is not to be ascribed to one's inadequacy, but to the defectiveness of the social order. The malcontent expects from the overthrow of the latter the success that the existing system has withheld from him. Consequently, it is entirely futile to try to make clear to him that the utopia he dreams of is not feasible and that the only foundation possible for a society organized on the principle of the division of labor is private ownership of the means of production. The neurotic clings to his "saving lie," and when he must make the choice of renouncing either it or logic, he prefers to sacrifice logic.[12]

It turns out, then, that the main difficulty confronting liberalism in gaining acceptance of its program is not the irrationality of the masses but, rather, the neurosis of a few influential people. These people are the "intellectuals" who furnish the masses with their ideas and ideology. The masses always seek a short cut for thought, and the real danger to the liberal order comes from the originators of such ideological short cuts. Even the intelligent layman, who ponders these questions carefully, cannot expect to make an impact on the intellectual establishment because

in all these discussions the professionals have an advantage over the laymen. The odds are always in favor of those who devote all their effort exclusively to one thing only. . . . Now, almost all these professionals are zealous advocates of bureaucratism and socialism. There are, first of all, the hosts of employees of the governments' and the various parties' propaganda offices. There are furthermore the teachers of various educational institutions which curiously enough consider the avowal of bureaucratic, socialist, or Marxian radicalism the mark of scientific perfection. There are the editors and contributors of "progressive" newspapers and magazines, labor-union leaders and organizers, and finally leisured ambitious men anxious to get into the headlines by the expression of radical views. The ordinary businessman, lawyer, or wage earner is no match for them.

The layman may brilliantly succeed in proving his argument. It is of no use. For his adversary, clothed with the full dignity of his office or his professorship, shouts back: "The fallacy of the gentleman's reasoning has long since been unmasked by the famous German professors, Mayer, Müller, and Schmid. Only an idiot can still cling to such antiquated and done-for ideas." The layman is discredited in the eyes of the audience, fully trusting in professional infallibility. He does not know how to answer.[13]

Thus, it is the intellectuals who make the thoughtlessness of the masses a danger. Modern advocates of aristocracy (such as José Ortega y Gasset) blame the degeneracy of the times on the boorishness of the lower classes whose emancipation, via democracy, is really the triumph of the new type of dictatorship—the dictatorship of the majority. But the real danger is not the masses but the intellectual elite that persuades them to adopt antiliberal causes. Mises explained:

Who is responsible for the deplorable events of the last decades? Did perhaps the lower classes, the proletarians, evolve the new doctrines? Not at all. No proletarian contributed anything to the construction of antiliberal teachings. . . .The overwhelming success of these doctrines which have proved so detrimental to peaceful social cooperation and now shake the foundations of our civilization is not an outcome of lower-class activities. The proletarians, the workers, and the farmers are certainly not guilty. Members of the upper classes were the authors of these destructive ideas. The intellectuals converted the masses to this ideology; they did not get it from them. If the supremacy of those modern doctrines is a proof of intellectual decay, it does not demonstrate that the lower strata have conquered the upper ones. It demonstrates rather the decay of the intellectuals and of the bourgeoisie. The masses, precisely because they are dull and mentally inert, have never created new ideologies. This has always been the prerogative of the elite. The truth is that we face the degeneration of a whole society and not an evil limited to some parts of it.[14]

According to Mises, not only were the classical liberals strategically naive about the ability of the masses to grasp the rationality of their arguments, but they were mistaken in considering institutions like "freedom" and "peace" and "private property" to be separate ideals. They failed to understand that "freedom" and "peace" are not ethical abstractions but the consequence of property institutions. The early liberal theorists reasoned that man was "free" because either God or Nature, abhorring slavery, had given each individual personal autonomy. Such arguments, Mises claimed, are completely superfluous to the conclusions of modern *scientific* liberalism. The question of natural and divine providence is metaphysical and not one that science can even attempt to answer. Mises made this comment on the separate tasks of metaphysics and science:

[I]t is no part of the task of science to examine ultimate questions or to prescribe values and determine their order of rank. Nevertheless, one may call the fulfillment of these tasks higher, nobler, and more important than that of the simpler task of science, which is to develop a theoretical system of cause-and-effect relationships enabling us to arrange our action in such a way that we can attain the goals we aim at. . . .Metaphysics and science perform different functions. They cannot, therefore, adopt the same procedures, nor are they alike in their goals. They can work side by side without enmity because they need not dispute each other's domain as long as they do not misconstrue their own character.[15]

The only time a conflict develops between metaphysics and science "is when one or the other attempts to overstep the boundary between them."[16] This happens when metaphysics (in the form of a "philosophy of history") decides to alter the character of some positive science like economics, or when science (in the form of "positivism") decides to abolish metaphysics and therefore becomes metaphysical itself. Without being "metaphysical" or even becoming embroiled in moral argument, modern liberalism seems to be able to make a value-free case for freedom. For example, modern liberalism's attack on slavery consists in demonstrating that the slave is necessarily less productive than the free worker; hence, slavery is undesirable because it is inefficient. In Mises words:

When those who recommended the abolition of involuntary servitude on general humanitarian grounds were told that the retention of the system was also in the interest of the enslaved, they knew of nothing to say in rejoinder. For against this objection in favor of slavery there is only *one* argument that can and did refute all others—namely, that free labor is incomparably more productive than slave labor. The slave has no interest in exerting himself fully. He works only as much and as zealously as is necessary to escape the punishment attaching to failure to perform the minimum. The free worker, on the other hand, knows that the more his labor accomplishes, the more he will be paid. . . .We liberals do not assert that God or Nature meant all men to be free, because we are not instructed in the designs of God and of Nature, and we avoid, on principle, drawing God and Nature into a dispute over mundane questions. What we maintain is only that a system based on freedom for all workers warrants the greatest productivity of human labor and is therefore in the interests of all the inhabitants of the earth. We attack involuntary servitude, not in spite of the fact that it is advantageous to the "masters," but because we are convinced that, in the last analysis, it hurts the interests of all members of human society, including the "masters."[17]

According to Mises, individual freedom is inextricably linked with the market economy. Only the conditions of a commercial economy offer the individual the greatest freedom possible. Mises explained this point as follows:

Liberty and freedom are the conditions of man within a contractual society. . . .The member of a contractual society is free because he serves others only in serving himself. What restrains him is only the inevitable natural phenomenon of scarcity. For the rest he is free in the range of the market. There is no kind of freedom and liberty other than the kind which the market economy brings about.[18]

Let us attempt to interpret Mises' reasoning. Freedom is the condition of the relative independence of my will from the will of others, or, stated another way, the relative independence of my plans from the plans of others. The freedom enjoyed by the individual cannot be judged by his experiences in a given society, where, in fact, he may feel quite frustrated. Rather that freedom must be judged by comparing his present state with the autonomy he would enjoy under some alternative social arrangement. On the basis of this intersocietal comparison the situation of the actor in a market-oriented society turns out to be superior on every count to that of the actor in a command or socialistic society. The decentralized planning of the market offers a greater probability of success than "societal" planning on a centralized or command basis. In a market situation, the individual's plans are not subject to the plans of any one person or even a few persons: the individual conforms to the plans of others because he thereby advances his own. The market not only provides the individual with the autonomy needed to carry out his plans but also offers information about the plans of others by way of the pricing mechanism. Such knowledge is hard to procure in a society where the outcome of action is uncertain because it is subject to the whims and arbitrary decisions of a centralized Planning Board.

Mises' claim that positive science can be separated from metaphysics and that the former can independently provide arguments in favor of liberty is not completely convincing. Certainly, the conclusion that a harmony of social interests exists in the market requires that a master science arrange a hierarchical ordering of subordinate sciences to insure that the findings of different disciplines do not conflict. For Mises, *epistemology* functions as this master science. Yet epistemology is metaphysical in some respects. We may wonder if Mises' abandonment of a "moral" approach to justifying freedom is not based on utilitarian grounds, that is, the case for freedom is best argued when one shows its ultimate usefulness. But the arguments in support of totalitarian ideologies do employ nonutilitarian augumentation, and this may explain their triumph over liberalism. Thus the pragmatic approach to liberty, which Mises advocated, may not be so effective (or utilitarian) as Mises himself supposed. On the other hand, there is some merit in Mises' position. There is no need for justice and expediency to be conflicting goals. If Mises' analysis of the usefulness of the market is correct, the reason may be that the market is compatible with an important human attribute; for surely human nature is the ultimate source of all moral reasoning. The same humanness that gives rise to the positive science of economics must provide clues as to how men ought to act, and that "ought" may well bolster the claims of liberal economists. Certainly, Mises should not rule out the importance of ethical analyses when arguing the case for the market.

Finally, we come to the concept of "equality," which, according to Mises, was wrongly understood by the early liberal thinkers. The classical liberal theorists believed that

God created all men equal, endowing them with fundamentally the same capabilities and talents, breathing into all of them the breath of His spirit. All distinctions between men are only artificial, the product of social, human—that is to say, transitory—institutions. What is imperishable in man—the spirit—is undoubtedly the same in rich and poor, noble and commoner, white and colored.[19]

In reality, however, men are "altogether unequal" with regard to their physical and other attributes, and therefore any argument for equal treatment under the law will not be convincing if it is based on the incorrect premise that individuals are equally talented or possess an alleged philosophically discoverable common humanity. With equal treatment under the law in a market economy, individual differences are so utilized as to promote each individual's private interests. Mises wrote:

There are two distinct reasons why all men should receive equal treatment under the law. One was already mentioned when we analyzed the objections to involuntary servitude. . . .The second consideration in favor of the equality of all men under the law is the maintenance of social peace. It has already been pointed out that every disturbance of the peaceful development of the division of labor must be avoided. But it is well-nigh impossible to preserve lasting peace in a society in which the rights and duties of the respective classes are different. Whoever denies rights to a part of the population must always be prepared for a united attack by the disenfranchised on the privileged. Class privileges must disappear so that the conflict over them may cease.[20]

Liberalism is revolutionary insofar as it challenges the legal privileges of the few in nonmarket forms of society such as feudalism and socialism. Mises' defense of the particular notion of "equality under the law" is the basis of his support of democracy. Democracy, for Mises, is the political arrangement consistent with a society based on unregulated commercial exchange. The election and dismissal of public officials by majority vote is the only political arrangement that makes revolution itself unnecessary. Mises explained:

Civil War and revolution are the means by which the discontented majorities overthrow rulers and methods of government which do not suit them. For the sake of domestic peace liberalism aims at democratic government. Democracy is therefore not a revolutionary institution. On the contrary, it is the very means of preventing revolutions and civil wars. It provides a method for the peaceful adjustment of government to the will of the majority. When the men in office and their policies no longer please the majority, they will—in the next election—be eliminated and replaced by other men espousing different policies.

The principle of majority rule or government by the people as recommended by liberalism does not aim at the supremacy of the mean, of the lowbred, of the domestic barbarians. The liberals too believe that a nation should be ruled by those best fitted for this task. But they believe that a man's ability to rule proves itself better by convincing his fellow-citizens than by using force upon them.[21]

According to Mises, liberalism is necessarily opposed to anarchism: "[T]he liberal understands quite clearly that without resort to compulsion, the existence of society would be endangered and that behind the rules of conduct whose observance is necessary to assure peaceful human cooperation must stand the threat of force, if the whole edifice of society is not to be continually at the mercy of one of its members."[22] But the logical extension of Mises' defense of liberalism may, in fact, point the way to anarchism. Why cannot any minority suddenly claim to be the majority by a geographical redefinition of the electorate? Anarchism need not endorse a belief in man's natural goodness or even a belief in utopian pacifism, as Mises apparently supposed. Anarchism may be a corollary of Mises' own belief in self-determination—something that he himself considered more important than majority rule:

The right of self-determination in regard to the question of membership in a state thus means: whenever the inhabitants of a particular territory, whether it be a single village, a whole district, or a series of adjacent districts, make it known, by a freely conducted plebiscite, that they no longer wish to remain united to the state to which they belong at the time, but wish either to form an independent state or to attach themselves to some other state, their wishes are to be respected and complied with. This is the only feasible and effective way of preventing revolutions and civil and international wars.[23]

Mises explained that he was not referring to *national* self-determination but jurisdictional self-determination, or, in his words, "the right of self-determination of the inhabitants of every territory large enough to form an independent administrative unit."[24] This implies that *individual* self-determination, or anarchism, is ruled out only on technical grounds, because if it were feasible, anarchism would be preferable to democracy:

If it were in any way possible to grant this right of self-determination to every individual person, it would have to be done. This is impractical only because of compelling technical considerations, which make it necessary that a region be governed as a single administrative unit and that the right to self-determination be restricted to the will of the majority of the inhabitants of areas large enough to count as territorial units in the administration of the country.[25]

Mises, then, opened himself up to the claims of the individualist anarchists, who believe such a radical self-determination not only feasible but, on Mises' own grounds, the ultimate source of social peace. It is interesting that the ground for this whole discussion has shifted from considerations of *utility* to considerations of *rights*. At this point Mises' position is weakened by the old problem of consent versus wisdom. If, say, a Nazi majority wishes to secede from a liberal state and exterminate the unfortunate members of the inferior race within its borders, Mises would probably oppose this act of secession. But to do so would sacrifice the criterion of geographical expediency to that of universal rights.

Mises' notion of "equality," then, is not connected with equality of condition but with equality of opportunity. Mises was concerned with means rather than ends. His political philosophy is a species of the ethics of constraint rather than of "end realization." To treat men equally under the law, as Hayek has demonstrated,[26] is to permit unequal results insofar as each human actor starts from a position of inequality with regard to talent and opportunity. To bring about an equality of status among men necessarily requires that they be treated unequally before the law. Both notions of equality cannot be pursued simultaneously, and each pursuit is characteristic of opposite political regimes. Mises summed up the modern liberal case for equality in terms of the notion of equal treatment before the law and characteristically insisted that the liberal case must be argued on utilitarian grounds:

It is therefore quite unjustifiable to find fault with the manner in which liberalism put into effect its postulate of equality, on the ground that what it created was *only* equality before the law, and not real equality. Men are and will always remain unequal. It is sober considerations of utility such as those we have here presented that constitute the argument in favor of the equality of all men under the law.[27]

This comparison of Mises' version of liberalism with the liberalism of his eighteenth- and nineteenth-century forebears reveals that Mises contributed to a radical and new understanding of what liberalism means in terms of political philosophy. As a political creed, liberalism seeks the common good:

The question whether a certain institutional arrangement is or is not to be regarded as a privilege granted to a certain group, class, or person is not to be decided by whether or not it is advantageous to that group, class, or person, but according to how beneficial to the general public it is considered to be. . . .It is not on behalf of property owners that liberalism favors the preservation of the institution of private property. It is not because the abolition of that institution would violate property rights that the liberals want to preserve it. If they considered the abolition of the institution of private property to be in the general interest, they would advocate that it be abolished, no matter how prejudicial such a policy might be to the interests of property owners.[28]

The defense of private property now has a utilitarian foundation, and a commitment to liberty, equality, and peace follows as a by-product of private property. The logical foundation for these assertions is contained in Mises' magnum opus, *Human Action: A Treatise on Economics*. Mises described how his understanding of economics was much broader than that of the older nineteenth-century writers because it was based on the notion of man as a "choosing" rather than a "selfish" agent:

Until the late nineteenth century political economy remained a science of the "economic" aspects of human action, a theory of wealth and selfishness. It dealt with human action only to the extent that it is actuated by what was—very unsatisfactorily—described as the profit motive, and it asserted that there is in addition other human action whose treatment is the task of other disciplines. The transformation of thought which the classical economists had initiated was brought to its consummation only by modern subjectivist economics, which converted the theory of market prices into a general theory of human choice.[29]

To be a human being, Mises argued, is to have a will, and having a will implies the ability to chose between alternative courses of action. If there is a science dedicated to the science of choice, that science is the master science of which economics is but one part. Mises named "praxeology" the "science of choice" and declared the science of economics to be but one part of "praxeology." Men's choices involve the application of scarce means to alternative ends. Economics is concerned with the way reason applies (scarce) means to alternative ends but does not address itself to the reasonableness of the ends themselves. According to Mises, action is always rational from the standpoint of the actors involved, and the scientist studying the forms of human action is entitled to take no other position:

Action is, by definition, always rational. One is unwarranted in calling goals of action irrational simply because they are not worth striving for from the point of view of one's own valuations. Such a mode of expression leads to gross misunderstandings. Instead of saying that irrationality plays a role in action, one should accustom oneself to saying merely: There are people who aim at different ends from those that I aim at, and people who employ different means from those I would employ in their situation.[30]

According to Mises, economics as an a priori science provides men with a set of cognitive categories for viewing the actions of others. By viewing economics as the science of human action carried out under conditions of scarcity, Mises declared that there is no sphere of human activity not subject to economic analysis: Economics is "the science of every kind of human action. Choosing determines all human decisions. In making his choice man chooses not only between various material things and services. All human values are offered for option."[31] Thus it necessarily follows that politics is one area where economic analysis can be applied:

Even the state and the legal system, the government and its administration are not too lofty, too good, too grand, for us to bring them within the range of rational deliberation. Problems of social policy are problems of social technology, and their solution must be sought in the same ways and by the same means that are at our disposal in the solution of other technical problems: by rational reflection and by examination of given conditions.[32]

Thus with the discovery of subjectivist economics even the political realm of social phenomena is open to praxeological investigation. But such a scientific inquiry into politics is also a political project; the investigation of the public good by an economist cannot but serve as a critique of existing political practices. And, of course, this critique is but the other side of Mises' positive defense of liberalism as being the best possible polity. According to Mises, the relationship between the new science of action and liberalism is a direct one: "One cannot understand liberalism without a knowledge of economics. For liberalism is applied economics; it is social and political policy based on a scientific foundation."[33]

The political program of liberalism is, therefore, the structuring or maintaining of a social order based on private ownership of the means of production. This entails, at the very least, the curbing of the power of the government, because private property is incompatible with governmental arbitrariness. The utility of private property lies precisely in the fact of decentralization and therefore the more efficient use of knowledge than is possible when resources are directed by centralized state planning. The liberal regime, according to Mises, is one in which political power is kept to a minimum:

As the liberal sees it, the task of the state consists solely and exclusively in guaranteeing the protection of life, health, liberty, and private property against violent attacks. Everything that goes beyond this is an evil. A government that, instead of fulfilling its task, sought to go so far as actually to infringe on personal security of life and health, freedom, and property would, of course, be altogether bad.[34]

The policies of the liberal regime are similar in their domestic and foreign application: the pursuit of freedom and peace through the protection of the domestic market and through the policy of international free trade. The enemies of liberalism are the various forms of *statism,* in particular, socialism and the half-way house of the bureaucratic welfare state. The welfare state tries to combine two incompatible approaches to solve economic problems. But the attempt to reconcile "command" and the market system eventually collapses into socialism proper. Mises stated that:

Every examination of the different conceivable possibilities of organizing society on the basis of the division of labor must always come to the same result: there is only the choice between communal ownership and private ownership of the means of production. All intermediate forms of social organization are unavailing and, in practice, must prove self-defeating. If one further realizes that socialism too is unworkable, then one cannot avoid acknowledging that capitalism is the only feasible system of social organization based on the division of labor. . . .A return to the Middle Ages is out of the question if one is not prepared to reduce the population to a tenth or a twentieth part of its present number and, even further, to oblige every individual to be satisfied with a modicum so small as to be beyond the imagination of modern man.[35]

In conclusion, we may say that the political thought of Ludwig von Mises represents an attempt to escape from the difficulties of the classical liberal position but that it is not without difficulties of its own. While Mises' insights into problems of applied economics are of great significance in instructing modern governments about how the material gains already won by capitalism are not to be lost, his prescriptions regarding notions of "equality" and "liberty" are defective in several respects. On the moral problems of a commercial economy Hayek's examination of the concept of the "rule of law" seems a more adequate confrontation with the phenomena than does Mises' complete disavowal of interest in "metaphysical issues."[36] The solution to the problem of justifying private property must reduce itself to questions of justice, as Murray N. Rothbard has pointed out.[37] It is precisely Hayek's concern with justice that marks him as a more suitable candidate than Mises for the title of the modern political philosopher of liberalism. Yet Hayek's definitions also suffer from the same formalistic difficulties that are found in Mises: neither offers us a substantive theory of liberty based upon a consideration of terms like "freedom" and "justice." The ultimate question presented by Mises and still left unanswered is whether we can ever arrive at a theory of society that is value free. Mises' attempt to offer such a theory was a bold one and went as far in the direction of utilitarianism as perhaps it is possible to go. But, as Aristotle noted in the fifth book of his *Politics*, it is not only the masses who ferment revolution but the elite as well. The masses are spurred on by a sense of outrage based upon oppression and a desire for equality. The better sort of men have higher motives—they revolt because of loftier issues like "justice" and "honor." Liberalism will succeed, according to Hayek, if it has ideals, but ideals are linked to a philosophical form of reasoning that Mises wished to avoid. The theory of the liberal state cannot be complete unless or until the moral side of liberalism is reexamined. Liberal theory simply will not succeed in redirecting civilization toward the old liberal program unless questions of an ethical sort are viewed as more fundamental than questions of economics. The battle against statism must not be fought in terms of "efficiency" alone if the entire war is to be won!

NOTES

1. Mises wrote, "The political antagonisms of today are not controversies over ultimate questions of philosophy, but opposing answers to the question how a goal that all acknowledge as legitimate can be achieved most quickly and with the least sacrifice. This goal, at which all men aim, is the best possible satisfaction of human wants; it is prosperity and abundance. Of course, this is not all men aspire to, but it is all they can expect to attain by resort to external means and by way of social cooperation. The inner blessings—happiness, peace of mind, exaltation—must be sought by each man within himself alone" (*The Free and Prosperous Commonwealth* [Princeton: D. Van Nostrand, 1962], p. 192).

2. Ibid., pp. 7-8; cf. Friedrich A. Hayek, *The Constitution of Liberty* (Chicago: Henry Regnery, 1972), p. 52.

3. Mises, *Free and Prosperous Commonwealth*, p. 3.

4. Ibid., p. 3.

5. Ibid., p. 157-58.

6. Ibid., p. 161.

7. Ludwig von Mises, *Omnipotent Government* (New Haven: Yale University Press, 1944), p. iii.

8. Mises, *Free and Prosperous Commonwealth*, pp. 164-65.

9. Ibid., p. 166.

10. Ludwig von Mises, *The Anti-Capitalistic Mentality* (Princeton: D. Van Nostrand, 1956).

11. Mises, *Free and Prosperous Commonwealth*, p. 14.

12. Ibid., p. 16.

13. Ludwig von Mises, *Bureaucracy* (New Haven: Yale University Press, 1962), p. 116.

14. Mises, *Omnipotent Government,* pp. 118-19.

15. Ludwig von Mises, *Epistemological Problems of Economics* (New York: D. Van Nostrand, 1960), p. 49.

16. Ibid.

17. Mises, *Free and Prosperous Commonwealth*, pp. 21-22.

18. Ludwig von Mises, *Human Action: A Treatise on Economics* (Chicago: Henry Regnery, 1966), pp. 282-83.

19. Mises, *Free and Prosperous Commonwealth*, pp. 27-28.

20. Ibid., p. 28.

21. Mises, *Human Action*, p. 150.

22. Mises, *Free and Prosperous Commonwealth*, p. 37.

23. Ibid., p. 109.

24. Ibid.

25. Ibid., pp. 109-10.

26. Hayek, *Constitution of Liberty*, pp. 85-102.

27. Mises, *Free and Prosperous Commonwealth*, pp. 28-29.

28. Ibid., pp. 29-30.

29. Mises, *Human Action*, p. 3.

30. Mises, *Epistemological Problems of Economics*, p. 35.

31. Mises, *Human Action*, p. 3.

32. Mises, *Free and Prosperous Commonwealth*, p. 71.

33. Ibid., p. 195.

34. Ibid., p. 52.

35. Ibid., pp. 85-86.

36. Hayek, *Constitution of Liberty*, pp. 162-75.

37. Murray N. Rothbard, *Power and Market: Government and the Economy* (Menlo Park, Calif.: Institute for Humane Studies, 1970), pp. 151-88.

Critical Discussion of the

Four Papers

Karen I. Vaughn

I am confronted here with an impossible task: to discuss four interesting and complex papers in no more than twenty minutes. The task is even more formidable when one considers that the link connecting these papers is not the unity of a single subject or a single theme, but rather the evaluation of the life's work of a man who, during the course of his lifetime, considered virtually every aspect of the science of economics. In a century in which reputations are built on short articles written on highly specialized parts of subfields in economics, Ludwig von Mises produced a comprehensive treatise on the whole science of human action, of which economics was the most developed part. Hence we have heard today four papers dealing with the contributions of Mises to our knowledge of economic action, each on a topic that occupies many volumes of economic literature. Although the topics are themselves very different—monetary theory, capital theory, economic calculation, and finally political philosophy—I shall try in the course of my comments to find some common themes that mark the thought of Ludwig von Mises.

First we turn to Professor Moss' paper on Mises' monetary theory. This is a suitable place to begin, since Mises' earliest and best known work was done in this field, although the value of his contributions has not always been appreciated. Professor Moss has done an excellent job of beginning to overcome this lack of appreciation. The Moss paper is by far the most ambitious and most

101

successful of the four papers, because Moss has gone beyond mere exposition of Mises' thought to critical evaluation and assessment of its relevance to contemporary economic theory. Too often it has been the practice of Austrians to emphasize their differences with received doctrine at the cost of ignoring the similarities. This was true of Carl Menger (although undoubtedly for very good reasons), it was true of Mises, and it is true of present-day Austrians. Mises especially was prone to stress the differences, often in a polemical and sometimes superficial manner, which, to say the least, frequently led to a lack of appreciation for the real subtlety of his arguments. To illustrate my point, I am reminded of something that happened this summer. Milton Friedman (a vocal and confirmed non-Austrian who nevertheless shares most of their policy conclusions) was invited to speak on Austrian economics to a group that had gathered for a week-long conference in Vermont. Professor Friedman proceeded to unendear himself to the gathering by proclaiming that, as far as he was concerned, there was no such thing as Austrian economics, only good economics and bad economics. To which most of the disgruntled audience felt compell-ed to reply, yes, but Austrian economics is good economics, and you just don't know about it. Hence, we appreciate Professor Moss' attempt to explain Mises in the terminology of modern economic theory, and we find as a result that the relationship between Mises' work and accepted mainstream economics is more often one of complementarity than of substitutability.

I take for my theme in discussing the Moss paper, Mises' emphasis on adjustment processes in the marketplace. Mises throughout his work was interested in how markets adjust to changing data, how information is transmitted, and how expec-tations are formed. This preoccupation is especially evident (and especially complementary to accepted doctrine) in two points dis-cussed by Moss. The first is the treatment of Mises' theory of how optimal cash balances are arrived at and how they are related to price levels. According to Moss, the problem Mises was trying to solve was the following: the optimum level of individuals' cash balances depends upon the price level, but the price level depends in part on the level of cash balances people choose to hold. How, then, can people arrive at their optimum cash balance without knowing the price level, which can only be determined after people decide how much cash to hold? Moss referred to this as the famous "circularity problem" that troubled early twentieth-century economic theory. Moss credited Patinkin with showing that the problem is eliminated once we realize that the optimum level of cash balances can be determined by the intersection of the supply curve for money and the demand curve derived by a hypothetical comparison of various price levels and the resulting level of cash balances desired, yet he congratulated Mises for developing a "bold empirical hypothesis" about how expectations are formed. Here is, I think, a perfect example of the importance of Mises' approach to economics as a supplement to neoclassical theory. Mises could not divorce the problem of the acquisition of knowledge and the formation of expectations from the problem of how equilibrium states are reached. While Patinkin was interested in defining an equilibrium condition, Mises was much more interested in explaining how human actions lead toward that equilibrium. In that light, Mises' hypothesis—that individuals determine their cash balances on the basis of yesterday's prices, which in turn affect today's prices, until expectations about prices and the actual price level converge to an equilibrium price is where the supply and demand curves intersect; justs from one equilibrium to another. Individual economic actors only know when the system is out of equilibrium, when reality does not meet their expectations (yet their expectations will have some influence on the reality that occurs), and it is this lack of realization of their plans that conveys the knowledge to them that they must revise their plans. It is this process that Mises was describing. We all tell our undergraduates that it is not enough to say that equilibrium price is where the supply and demand curves intersect; one must explain how that equilibrium is achieved and how the market adjusts to new equilibria. If we recognize that Patinkin told us what the equilibrium conditions are, it is Mises who was trying to explain how we get there.

This emphasis on processes of adjustment in the marketplace is also evident in what Moss called the "proportionality theorem." Here Mises' insistence on the importance of examining how inflation takes place adds far more to our understanding of the role of money in the economy that the simple statement that an increase in the quantity of money will cause the price level to rise. Mises, so to speak, filled in the gap between an increase in M and an increase in P and showed that not only the change in the quantity of money but also the route by which it enters the system are important in determining the ultimate course of inflation. In this analysis Mises went far beyond the "quantity theorists" upon whose theories he built. We might note that the analysis of the process of inflation was first attempted by Richard Cantillon in the eighteenth century, who was also attempting to ascertain who the gainers are and who the losers are from inflation. We can thank Mises for reviving and expanding an important analysis, which unfortunately was shunted aside in the nineteenth century.

Mises' concern with disequilibrium processes, with how expectations are formulated and how information is transmitted, all arose from his insistence on viewing economics exclusively as a science of individual action. While methodological individualism was not born in Mises' writings, it certainly was nurtured there with a dedication duplicated by few other economists. This methodological individualism is, I believe, the key to understanding Mises' view of capital and interest.

Professor Kirzner chose to explore one of the most difficult aspects of Misesian economics or any kind of economics for that matter. The theory of capital is perhaps the most controversial and least understood part of economic science; rarely in the literature does one find two economists who agree on what capital is and how it is measured, let alone how it functions in an economic system. We agree that we are better off with more of it than with less of it, but we are not exactly sure why. Into this area of confusion, Mises brought, if not total illumination, at least a consistency that is frequently lacking in the mainstream literature.

Professor Kirzner did an admirable job of clarifying some of the more difficult aspects of Mises' theory of capital by contrasting Mises' views with those of Bohm-Bawerk (whom most of us generally take to be the quintessential Austrian capital theorist) and Frank Knight, the leader of the opposing camp. We come to realize that, because of Mises' concern with the individual as the only acting entity, the entire concept of capital is relevant only to individual decision making, an attitude that is evident in Mises' distinction between capital and capital goods. *Capital goods* are unfinished consumer goods, which are arranged from higher order to lower order depending upon how close they are to the finished product. Because they are a heterogeneous grouping of unfinished goods, only the entrepreneur is able to decide what is and what is not a capital good, and that decision depends upon his plans for their future use (a can of beans on a grocer's shelf is only a capital good if the grocer plans to sell it rather than to eat it himself). *Capital,* on the other hand, is purely an accounting concept and is equal to the market value of all assets minus the market value of liabilities of a business organization. It is useful only as a means of calculating the profitability of an enterprise and of aiding the entrepreneur in his decision making. There is no meaning to a concept of an aggregate capital stock since one cannot aggregate a collection of heterogeneous entities. Also there is no meaning to the idea of an aggregate fund of capital since the market value of the existing group of unfinished goods is subject to continual change as the unfolding of entrepreneurial plans reveals unanticipated conflicts that nullify the expectations of some and exceed the expectations of others. Hence, the attempt to arrive at a calculation of the value of the capital stock of some political entity (say, the United States of America) yields only a meaningless number that says nothing about the level of income to be expected in the future, because it says nothing about the decision-making process of the owners and users of the capital.

It is perhaps astonishing to a neoclassical economist that Mises denied what is taken to be the mainstay of capital theory: the productivity of capital. Since capital goods are nothing but unfinished consumer goods, one cannot conceive of them as being productive in the way labor is productive. The factors of production to Mises are labor, land, and time. It takes human effort, material resources, and the passing of time to yield output. (If one may engage in a philosophical comment, this view of the primacy of human productive activity shows every bit as much of a respect for the "dignity of labor" as that one usually associated with Marxists, but for Mises all labor was important, including entrepreneurial labor.) Because Mises denied the productivity of capital, he also denied any role for capital productivity in the formation of the interest rate, which was instead the result of pure time preference. It is here that I wish Professor Kirzner had been a little more expansive. He stated that "the phenomenon of interest arises only because, as a result of time preference, factors reflect only the *discounted* values of their services." I think what Professor Kirzner meant here is that only time preference gives rise to a rate of interest in the sense that factors of production reflect only their discounted marginal value products. If capital goods were productive of future output, however, would not people still be willing to pay a premium to borrow money to invest in capital in the hope of receiving a greater return in the future whether or not they valued goods higher in the present than in the future? Perhaps the confusion here is mine rather than Professor Kirzner's, and I only wish he had dealt with this controversial problem at greater length.

Mises' theory of capital provides a good transition to the next paper on our program, Professor Rothbard's on Mises and the controversy over economic calculation under socialism, because the heart of the Misesian challenge was his contention that it would be impossible to calculate efficiently under socialism without capital markets to determine input prices. Rothbard's paper was also well placed in the program because the controversy about which he wrote summarizes Mises' view of the functioning of a market economy. To paraphrase Professor Rothbard, the controversy was much more than one over socialism versus capitalism as we know it, rather it was a controversy over the efficacy of political versus economic action. It is ironic that this is the one area discussed in the session where Mises was given glowing recognition for his achievement while it is generally believed that he lost the debate. I am reminded of Buchanan's statement that the degree to which one accepts the alleged defeat of Mises is the degree to which one is con-

fused as to what the debate was about. Though I think that
Professor Rothbard perhaps gave Mises too much credit for working out the details of the Austrian answer to the controversy about
economic calculation, when in fact it was Hayek who chose to res-
pond to some of the more difficult problems (Mises' so-called final
refutation in *Human Action* is mostly polemic and glosses over the
real problems), I admit that it was Mises, nevertheless, who indicated in what direction the answer to the Socialists lay.

The importance of the debate can, I believe, be underscored by a
remark Hayek once made to the effect that because of Mises the
Socialists were forced to change their claim that socialism was
superior to capitalism to a defense of the possibility of socialism at
all. Furthermore, to every challenge Mises and Hayek hurled at the
Socialist scheme, the response was to find some means of
duplicating the market. To Mises, this alone was evidence of his
triumph over the Socialists, since he considered every admission of
the need for markets to be one more step away from pure socialism.
To Mises, the final proposals of Lange were no longer socialism at
all but state capitalism, where the Planning Board assumed the entrepreneurial function and performed in a manner far inferior to the
decentralization of this function, which is characteristic of the free
market.

What I believe to be the most interesting results of the controversy, however, were the further developments of economic theory to
which it gave rise. For example, Rothbard noted the further
developments in the theory of cost as a subjective phenomenon
dependent solely on the forgone utility of the chooser, that took
place at the London School of Economics during the thirties,
forties, and fifties. This work grew out of an examination of the idea
of using the rule of marginal cost pricing to direct the behavior of
Socialist managers. Hayek, Coase, and Thirlby all questioned the
usefulness of such a rule if one accepts the idea that the evaluation
of cost is not merely a mechanical adding up of expenditures but
depends upon the ability of the manager to assess the value of
forgone opportunities with which he is confronted. Furthermore,
when the manager's judgments are to be monitored, not by the

profits or losses he earns in the market place, but by a Planning Board who must agree with his evaluation of costs, the manager's behavior is bound to differ substantially from that of the market entrepreneur.

This raises a most fundamental question involved in the Socialist controversy: what is the role of private ownership in economic activity? Mises and Hayek both believed that the essence of entrepreneurial activity was risk-taking in one's attempt to anticipate the market. If the users of capital were to be shielded even partially from the consequences of their risky actions (either good or bad), their actions would be far different from those of people who were risking their own fortunes regardless of the behavioral rules issued by the Planning Board. Hence central planning could never duplicate the outcomes of a functioning market economy.

Finally, we come to a consideration of Professor Baumgarth's paper, a fitting conclusion to our survey of the economic contributions of Ludwig von Mises, since Mises defended his politics of liberalism on economic grounds. I will address my comments to one particular aspect of Baumgarth's paper: the source of Mises' defense of liberalism.

Liberalism as a philosophy implies individual freedom. In the seventeenth century, when the philosophy was being developed in England, freedom was considered to be a value desirable for its own sake. It was a natural condition of human beings. (This positing of a natural condition was an attempt to find a "scientific" way of determining what political society should be. By starting with man in a state of nature one could then discover what role government should play in civil society.) It was a moral value that, as a bonus, also happened to lead to the well-being of society. The moral, or, as it was viewed at the time, the scientific, argument was primary, and the utilitarian argument was brought in as additional fire power. This was the way John Locke developed the philosophy of liberalism and the way it was understood until sometime in the nineteenth century. By the time of John Stuart Mill, however, the argument became reversed, and freedom was espoused, not because it was a good in itself, but because it led to "the greatest good for the greatest number." Obviously, if it could have been shown that the greatest good for the greatest number (assuming, of course, there is some way to define and recognize such a thing when one is confronted with it) was best achieved through restriction of individual liberty and control of man's economic activities, the case for freedom would be nullified. (This is, in fact, precisely what happened in the United States, where liberalism means exactly the opposite of what it meant in nineteenth-century England: here liberals are in favor of restriction of economic freedoms, which they perceive to be contrary to the greatest good for the greatest number.)

Mises, unfortunately, attempted to refute the collectivists and authoritarians by accepting the terms of their argument and arguing for the superior ability of the free market to provide for the economic well-being of the populace. We see this in the economic-calculation argument, where he took his demonstration of the superior efficiency of the market as a complete refutation of socialism as a political system. Such an attempt to defend freedom is dangerous on two counts. First, it is open to empirical refutation. For instance, Mises' attack on slavery was based on the contention that slavery is inefficient: yet the recent work of Fogel and Engerman suggests that, on the contrary, it is a highly efficient system if one does not count the loss of utility to the slaves. How then does one argue for freedom in this case? Secondly, the defense of freedom on utilitarian grounds is dangerous for a more important reason. Even given that the market is much more efficient at providing for the well-being of individuals in a material sense, this is not the final refutation of a political system, because there may be nonmaterial items in individual utility functions. For example, what about those individuals whose utility functions include the desire to control and regulate, whose skills are greatest in bureaucratic paper shuffling and carrying favor with higher-ups in the bureaucracy? Such people would not fare well in a completely free market (or at least they will do better in an environment that rewards such activity more highly than the market does), and their well-being will be greatly enhanced in a system predicated on control. Since no interpersonal comparisons of utility are permitted, which system will provide then for the maximum social welfare?

What this leads us to, I believe, is the conclusion that the justification for any political system, whether it be complete authoritarianism, anarchism, or something in between, must be based on more than just economic efficiency: it must include a moral justification, and this moral justification must be based on a system of ethics that can be shared by all rational human beings. Mises despaired that such a rational ethics might never be developed, but without it there cannot be a conclusive defense of freedom.

Closing Remarks

Fritz Machlup

Although the program lists me only as the chairman of this panel—and chairmen, as a rule, close a session by saying not much more than "thank you" to the participants—this time the chairman was asked by the organizers to serve also as a second discussion speaker. Professor Karen Vaughn has just done an excellent job of discussing the four papers. She did it with grace, intelligence, real understanding of the issues, and remarkable knowledge of the literature. Hence I feel a little superfluous; moreover, I have a propensity to leave the last word to a lady. These considerations, however, are counteracted by the thought that a liberated woman may not want to be treated as a lady and by my strong belief that promises should be kept. Thus I shall do what I have promised and make a few remarks on each of the four papers, even if some of my observations merely reinforce Professor Vaughn's pronouncements.

Professor Moss' paper deals with a large number of monetary problems. It is such a rich mine of interesting issues that I have a difficult time selecting one that I can discuss in but a few minutes. I choose to talk about some aspects of the demand for money, because this is where Mises probably made one of his greatest contributions. Later analysts have criticized Mises on a variety of points, though some have had the good sense of recognizing that pioneers should not be expected to come up with complete and accurately formulated statements of definitive findings. Some of the criticism has focused on the difference between the demand for *nominal* amounts of money and the demand for *real* balances. Let me invite you to think of a demand curve for holding money where we indicate (or plot) on the abscissa the nominal amounts of money and on the ordinate the purchasing power (real value) of a unit of money. If the horizontal distances show the amounts of money demanded for nominal balances, the rectangles inscribed under the curve, that is, the amounts of money multiplied by their real value, will show the real balances. If it is that easy to translate a demand curve for money balances into one for real balances, there can hardly be such a *fundamental* schism between the two theories.

The circularity problem was one that bothered many economists sixty years ago; that was before they fully comprehended the idea of mutual determination or interdependence. How could one explain general movements of prices by changes in the supply of, and demand for, money if one were blocked from grasping that the demand for money was in turn to be understood as a function of prices? We no longer see any difficulty with this type of interdependence, whether it be formulated in terms of a set of simultaneous equations or in terms of a sequence analysis of equilibrium positions. No doubt in 1911 the charge of circularity had to be taken seriously. That is the reason Mises resorted to a sequence analysis but interpreted it as a "historical link" between yesterday's prices and today's decisions. The term *historical* was a bit misleading, but the main thing was that the association of experience with expectations was established in the student's mind.

Of even greater significance was what Mises said about "abnormal situations," in which expectation of future price increases may not be formed just by the experiences with yesterday's prices but also by announcements and expectations of governmental fiscal and monetary policies. If prices are expected to increase—not because they have risen in the past, but because of announcements, reports, authoritative interpretations, rumors, or what not—the resulting decline in the demand for money may well lead to an actual rate of price increase far in excess of what could be explained by the ongoing increase in the supply of money. Indeed the resulting decline in aggregate real balances may provide a good description of what goes on during a galloping price inflation.

Kirzner's paper on Mises' views on capital and interest is a gem—lucid, beautiful, and elegant. But I shall not dismiss it with this sincere praise; for I want to point to a few issues where he correctly presents the master's view but fails to warn that it may not be the last word. I think Mises would have wanted us to express any doubts we might have regarding his propositions. I shall select two of the issues on which I would not want my students and grand-students to stick to my teacher's formulations, as if they presented the only tenable statement on the problems in question:

1. Time preference as a universal phenomenon: For Mises time preference was not an empirical regularity but a "definite categorial element . . . operative in every instance of action." Well, if time preference is seen as *positive* time preference, the claim that it is ever present in the decisions of each and every household may be true or false, and it is, therefore, an empirical proposition. On the other hand, since time preference may be large, small, zero, or even negative, we may assert that it is a universal characteristic of human action. If, when comparing present with future gratification, some individuals postpone consumption without the promise of a positive interest rate, their marginal rate of time preference is evidently zero. If, without receiving interest, they allocate their present and future availabilities in such a fashion that they may expect to consume equal amounts this year, next year, and in any future year, then their time preference in the schedule sense must be defined as being zero. But what the facts actually are remains an empirical question. People have different tastes, different incomes, different expectations of future income and needs, and different opportunities for trade-offs between present and future consumption.

2. The total capital stock: Mises was certainly correct when he objected to the ambiguous notion of a measurable stock of capital. Virtually all economists agree with this. He was also quite correct in distinguishing capital funds (money capital) and capital goods (real capital). And, again, he was correct in saying that anyone interested in a complete inventory taking of the totality of capital goods would have to resort to an enumeration of a huge pile of altogether different things, a compilation that would not be of any use to anyone. Incidentally, Böhm-Bawerk also rejected the relevance of the total of capital goods for problems of interest-rate determination and instead worked with the total of all goods and

resources. He realized that the length of time an economy can wait for future consumer goods to become available (in time-taking production processes) depends not only on "produced means of production" (i.e., capital goods) but also on the amount of non-perishable consumer goods and the future services of exhaustible and nonexhaustible resources. Of course, none of these aggregates plays any direct role in the considerations and plans of individual decision makers. However, this is true not only in capital theory but also in price theory in general, where the stocks of available goods play an indirect role in the decisions of any individual: the size of such stocks affects the decisions of individual households and firms by way of the price mechanism.

In Rothbard's paper on economic calculation under socialism, I was especially intrigued by his statement that the central Planning Board in its decision making—without market prices to aid its calculation—is in the same position as a big business firm or any organization that is vertically integrated to such a large degree that markets disappear or market prices can be disregarded. This is an issue that I have tried to sell in several of my publications (the first time in a book that appeared in 1934 and most recently in a paper on international integration,[1]) but unfortunately not with sufficient success. Whenever a firm (or concern) supplies the output of one of its departments as an input to another of its departments instead of selling it in a competitive market at a price established by supply and demand, the problem of artificial transfer prices or of jumbled cost-and-revenue figures arises. There may still be calculations, but not according to the economic principle—or what Mises termed "economic calculations."

The hope that large, vertically integrated firms will eventually disappear because they are inefficient and work with excessive production costs rests, I am sorry to say, on the assumption of degrees of competition that do not exist in our society. There may be cost advantages enabling the big firms to overcome the inefficiency of vertically integrated (and therefore "uneconomic") calculations and dispositions, and there may even be offsetting marketing advantages enabling them to survive and even to prosper and grow.

The last paper, by Baumgarth, is admirable in its careful selection of significant quotations in the attempt to show how Mises' conceptions of the liberal order all hang together. I want to make only a brief comment on terminology. For the benefits of less widely read students, what Mises called "classical liberalism" should be carefully distinguished from the names that its exponents may have given to their ideas. To be sure, no one can call himself a "classic"—this is left to later generations looking back to some creators of paradigms. More interesting, however, is that the nineteenth-century writers who expounded "classical liberalism" rarely, if ever, referred to themselves as "liberals." Nor did anyone at their time give them such a designation. They were regarded as progressives or radical reformers and given similar appellations. *Liberal* and *liberalism* were first used in Spain for a political party, and since that time these words have been used in a good many mutually contradictory meanings. We have only to think of "utilitarian liberalism," "rational liberalism," "individual liberalism," "organic liberalism" "modern liberalism," and "American liberalism" to see rather fundamental contradictions. The failure to guard against this kind of confusion has lead to what I called "fuzzy liberalism," which seems to be the prevalent species of liberalism in the United States.[2] I would not go so far as to say that the word *liberalism* was "stolen" by illiberal demagogues, but one may reasonably suspect that most self-styled "liberals" have been untroubled by any knowledge of the literature on the subject.

More could and should be said on this paper and on any of the other three. Unfortunately, time does not allow it. All that I have time for is to thank the speakers for their fine performances. This session, I think, has been interesting as well as valuable to anyone who cares about economic theory and economic philosophy. I feel that even Mises himself would have enjoyed it.

NOTES

1. Fritz Machlup, *Führer durch die Krisenpolitik* (Vienna: Julius Springer, 1934), pp. 209-14; in a French edition, *Guide à travers les panacées economiques* (Paris: Librairie de Médicis, 1938), pp. 309-16; in a most recent version, "Integrationshemmende Integrationspolitik," *Bernhard-Harms-Vorlesungen*, ed. Herbert Giersch (Kiel: Institut für Weltwirtschaft, Universitat Kiel, 1974), pp. 42-45, 52-54.

2. Fritz Machlup, "Liberalism and the Choice of Freedoms," in *Roads to Freedom*, ed. Erich Streissler (London: Routledge & Kegan Paul, 1969), pp. 117-46.

Appendices

APPENDIX A
Chronology

1881   September 29. Born in Lemberg, Austria. Father, Arthur Edler von Mises. Mother, Adele (Landau) von Mises. Brother, Richard von Mises (1883-1953).

1892-1900   Attended Akademische Gymnasium, Vienna.

1900   Entered University of Vienna to study for a degree in law.

1906   February 20. Received doctor of jurisprudence degree (literally, doctor of both, canon and roman, laws).

1902   First book published, *Die Entwicklung des gutsherrlich-bäuerlichen Verhaltnisses in Galizien: 1772-1848* (Leipzig: Franz Deuticke, 1902); a historical account of the Galician peasants and their land tenure arrangements.

1902-3   Active duty with the Austro-Hungarian army.

1909-34   Economic councillor of the Austrian Chamber of Commerce (Kammer für Handel, Gewerte und Industrie). Mises' chamber appraised legislation and advised the government on public policy.

1912   Published *Theorie des Geldes und der Umlaufsmittel* (translated in 1934 as *Theory of Money and Credit*); most important work on monetary theory.

1913   Appointed "professor extraordinary" at University of Vienna.

1914-18   Active military duty in World War I as captain in the artillery,
            stationed on Eastern Front in Carpathian Mountains, in Rus-
            sian Ukraine, and Crimea; toward end of war recalled to
            general staff office in Vienna.

1918-20   Director of Austrian Restitution-and-Settlements Office
            (Abrechnungs Amt).

1920   Published essay "Economic Calculation in the Socialist Com-
            monwealth."

1922   Published *Die Gemeinwirtschaft: Untersuchungen über den
            Sozialismus;* translated as *Socialism: An Economic and Sociological
            Analysis.*

1923   Published *Die Geldtheoretische Seite des Stabilisierungsproblems;* un-
            translated. See "Monetary Economics," note 1.

1926   Lecture tour of the United States under sponsorship of the
            Laura Spelman Rockefeller Memorial.

1927   Founded Austrian Institute for Business Cycle Research
            (Oesterreichisches Institut fur Konjunkturforschung).

1927   Published *Liberalismus;* translated as *The Free and Prosperous
            Commonwealth.*

1928   Published *Geldwertstabilisierung und Konjunkturpolitik;* un-
            translated. See "Monetary Economics," note 1.

1929   Published series of articles attacking various forms of state in-
            terventions: *Kritik des Interventionismus: Untersuchungen zur
            Wirtschaftspolitik und Wirtschaftsideologie der Gegenwart,* Jena:
            Gustav Fischer, 1929; untranslated.

1931   Published *Die Ursachen der Wirtschaftskrise: Ein Vortrag;* un-
            translated. See "Monetary Economics," note 1.

1933   Published *Grundprobleme der Nationalökonomie;* translated as
            Epistemological Problems of Economics.

1934-40 Accepted professorship at the Graduate Institute of International Studies (Institut Universitaire de Hautes Études Internationales) In Geneva, Switzerland.

1938 Married Margit Sereny-Herzfeld in Geneva.

1940 Immigrated to the United States; became a citizen in 1946.

1940-44 Guest of the National Bureau of Economic Research in New York.

1940 Published *Nationalökonomie: Theorie des Handelns und Wirtschaftens;* untranslated.

1942 Visiting professor at National University of Mexico.

1944 Published *Bureaucracy.*

1944 Published *Omnipotent Government.*

1945-69 Appointed visiting professor at Graduate School of Business Administration, New York University.

1946-73 Advisor to Foundation for Economic Education, Inc., Irvington-on-Hudson, New York.

1946 Consultant to National Association of Manufacturers—Economic Principles Commission.

1947 Co-founder of Mont Pelerin Society, an international association of intellectuals devoted to limited government and the market economy.

1949 Published *Human Action: A Treatise on Economics.*

1954-55 Advisor to the National Association of Manufacturers.

1956 Published *The Anti-Capitalist Mentality.*

1956 February 20. Awarded a *Festschrift* on the occasion of the 50th anniversary of his doctorate: *On Freedom and Free Enterprise.*

Edited by Mary Sennholz. Princeton: D. Van Nostrand, 1956.

1957   Published *Theory and History: An Interpretation of Social and Economic Evolution.*

1957   Awarded honorary doctor of laws degree, Grove City College, Pennsylvania.

1961   October. *Quarterly Journal* of Mont Pelerin Society published a tribute to Mises on the occasion of his 80th birthday.

1962   Published *The Ultimate Foundation of Economic Science: An Essay on Method.*

1962   October 20. Award received from Austrian Government (Oesterreichisches Ehrenzeichen zur Kunst und Wissenschaft).

1963   June. Awarded honorary doctor of laws degree from New York University, New York.

1964   July. Awarded honorary doctor of political science degree from University of Freiburg, Germany.

1969   September. Named "Distinguished Fellow" of American Economics Association. For citation see Introduction.

1969   Published *The Historical Setting of the Austrian School of Economics.*

1969   May. Retired from New York University.

1971   September 29. Honored on the occasion of his 90th birthday by a *Festschrift.* In two volumes: *Toward Liberty.* Edited by F. A. Hayek and other members of Mont Pelerin Society. Menlo Park, Calif.: Institute for Humane Studies, 1971.

1973   October 10. Died at 92 years of age.

APPENDIX B
Major Translated Writings of Ludwig von Mises

1912   *The Theory of Money and Credit.* Translated by H. E. Batson. New Haven: Yale University Press, 1959. The first German edition of this book appeared in 1912 under the title *Theorie des Geldes und der Umlaufsmittel.* For a discussion of the different editions of this book, see p. 40, note 1. This book is the subject of "The Monetary Economics of Ludwig von Mises" in this volume.

1920-21   "Economic Calculation in the Socialist Commonwealth." In *Collectivist Economic Planning: Critical Studies on the Possibilities of Socialism,* edited by Friedrich A. Hayek; translated by S. Adler. London: Routledge & Kegan, Paul, 1963. This article originally appeared under the title "Die Wirtschaftsrechnung im sozialistischen Gemeinwesen." *Archiv fur Sozialwissenschaft und Sozialpolitik* 47 (1920-21): 86-121. The main points of this article are treated in Murray N. Rothbard's paper "Ludwig von Mises and Economic Calculation under Socialism" in this volume.

1922   *Socialism: An Economic and Sociological Analysis.* Translated by J. Kahane. New Haven: Yale University Press, 1951. This translation is from the second German edition (1923), which included two articles by Mises: "Die Arbeit im sozialistischen Gemeinwesen. *Zeitschrift für Volkswirtschaft und Sozialpolitik* N. F. 1 (1921): 459-76; and "Neue Beiträge zum Problem der

For a comprehensive bibliography of Mises' writings, see Bettina Bien [Greaves], *The Works of Ludwig von Mises* (Irvington-on-Hudson, N.Y.: Foundation for Economic Education, 1969).

sozialistischen Wirtschaftsrechnung.'' *Archiv für Sozialwissenschaft und Sozialpolitik* 51 (1924): 488-500. The first edition of *Socialism* appeared under the title *Die Gemeinwirtschaft: Untersuchungen über den Sozialismus*. Jena: Gustav Fischer, 1922. As the title implies, Mises criticized the Socialist arguments from the point of view that the sociological and economic consequences of socialism are precisely the opposite of what is intended by the advocates of socialism. He also attacked the argument that socialism is historically necessary.

1927   *The Free and Prosperous Commonwealth: An Exposition of the Ideas of Classical Liberalism*. Translated by Ralph Raico. Princeton: D. Van Nostrand, 1962. This translation is from *Liberalismus*. Jena: Gustav Fischer, 1927. Here Mises restated the case for economic freedom on purely scientific grounds, that is, grounds that do not appeal to natural law or other metaphysical notions. William Baumgarth treats this book in his paper "Ludwig von Mises and the Justification of the Liberal Order" in this volume.

1933   *Epistemological Problems of Economics*. Translated by George Reisman. Princeton: D. Van Nostrand, 1960. This translation is from *Grundprobleme der Nationalökonomie: Untersuchungen über Verfahren, Aufgaben und Inhalt der Wirtschafts und Gesellschaftslehre*. Jena: Fustav Fischer, 1933. Here Mises emphasized how the distinctive feature of economics is its concern with subjective states of individual valuation. Mises explained how this approach affects the economist's view of value, capital, and other market phenomena. A large part of the work is spent criticizing the position of those who deny the subjective character of economic phenomena.

1944   *Omnipotent Government: The Rise of the Total State and Total War*. New Haven: Yale University Press, 1944. In this book Mises treated the concept of "nationalism" and how it invariably grows to block out cosmopolitan ideals of free trade and international peace. Mises' analysis of the rise of German Nazism, as a symptom of a more far-reaching mentality about government and its relation to man, serves as a warning about the dangerous risks that accompany departures from classical liberals ideals.

1944   *Bureaucracy*. New Haven: Yale University Press, 1962. This is one of the earliest works by an economist explaining the sources of bureaucratic inefficiency. According to Mises, it is the absence of "profit-and-loss" accounting that distinguishes bureaucratic management from entrepreneurial management.

1949   *Human Action: A Treatise on Economics*. 3d ed. rev. Chicago: Henry Regnery, 1966. As the title indicates, Mises took up the whole of the science of economics and explained it as a subset of the more general science of human action, which he termed "praxeology." The book is rich in its criticism of alternative schools of economic thought and philosophies of science that deny the unique and subjective character of the social sciences. The book is an expanded version of a German work: *Nationalökonomie: Theorie des Handelns und Wirtschaftens*. Geneva: Editions Union, 1940. Here Mises first argued the case for the praxeological character of the science. The second revised edition published by Yale University Press (1963) is marred by many serious typographical errors.

1952   *Planning for Freedom, and Other Essays and Addresses*. South Holland, Ill.: Libertarian Press, 1952. This is a collection of a dozen of Mises' most polemical writings, published in such libertarian publications as *The Freeman* and *Plain Talk*. All but one of the essays were written between 1945 and 1952. There is a more recent edition of this book by the same publisher in which Mises added an essay he had written in 1958. This edition appeared in 1962.

1956   *The Anti-Capitalistic Mentality*. Princeton: D. Van Nostrand, 1956. In this brief essay Mises analyzed the reasons why intellectuals find the capitalist system unacceptable. His search for the psychological roots of their criticism is touched on by Baumgarth in his paper "Ludwig von Mises and the Justification of the Liberal Order." Most of Mises' 1956 essay was reprinted in *U.S. News and World Report*, 19 October 1956.

1957   *Theory and History: An Interpretation of Social and Economic Evolution*. New Haven: Yale University Press, 1957. In this book Mises attacked the logical basis for believing that there are laws of social history analogous to the laws of the natural world. Mises also sketched his own theory of historical evolution, which is value free because it views historical phenomena as the outcome of purposive actions undertaken by individuals. A later edition was published by Arlington House in 1969.

1962   *The Ultimate Foundation of Economic Science: An Essay on Method.* Princeton: D. Van Nostrand, 1962. Here Mises argued that economic phenomena cannot be "explained" unless they are analyzed in terms of the choices and plans of acting individuals. This is the strongest case ever made for "methodological individualism" in economics.

1969   *The Historical Setting of the Austrian School of Economics.* New Rochelle, N.Y.: Arlington House, 1969. This is Mises' last published writing. It is a short essay recalling the struggle of the theoretical economists to gain acceptance of their point of view in the German universities, where the "historical school" of economists held a dominant and underserved position of academic (and therefore political) power.

Contributors to the Symposium on "The Economics of Ludwig von Mises," held before the 44th Meeting of the Southern Economics Association Atlanta, Georgia

15 November 1974

William Baumgarth was born on 10 July 1946 in Union City, New Jersey. He attended Fordham University, where he majored in political science, and graduated in 1968. He went on to Harvard University, where the Department of Government awarded him an M.A. in 1970. Baumgarth is scheduled to defend his dissertation, "The Political Philosophy of Friedrich von Hayek," before the Harvard faculty this summer (1975). He has contributed papers to the Libertarian Scholars Conference in New York City (1972) and to the Columbia University Forum on Legal and Political Philosophy (1974). His many academic awards and honors include membership in Phi Beta Kappa and being named a traveling Earhart Fellow while at Harvard. Baumgarth is an instructor of political science at Wake Forest University in North Carolina. This fall (1975) he will teach political philosophy in the Political Science Department of Fordham University, New York City.

Israel M. Kirzner was born on 13 February 1930 in London, England. He attended the University of Capetown (1947-48), University of London (1950-51), and Brooklyn College (1952-54), where he received his B.A. degree summa cum laude after majoring in economics. Kirzner went on to New York University, where he earned a master's degree in business administration in 1955 and a Ph.D. in economics in 1957. His dissertation advisor was Ludwig von Mises, and his dissertation was published under the title *The Economic Point of View* (New York: D. Van Nostrand, 1960). Kirzner attended Mises' economic theory seminar on a regular basis from 1954 to 1958. His other books are *Market Theory and the Price System* (New York: D. Van Nostrand, 1963), *An Essay on Capital* (New York: Augustus

127

M. Kelley, 1966), and most recently, *Competition and Entrepreneurship* (Chicago: University of Chicago Press, 1973). Kirzner is a professor of economics at New York University, New York City.

Fritz Machlup was born on 15 December 1902 in Wiener Neustadt, Austria. He earned his doctorate from the University of Vienna in 1923 and has been awarded honorary degrees on both sides of the Atlantic in recognition of his outstanding contributions to economics. He was a member of Ludwig von Mises' Vienna seminar during the twenties and went on to establish his reputation as one of Mises' most outstanding students. He served as president of the Southern Economics Association (1959-60), of the American Economic Association (1966), and of the International Economics Association (1971-74). He was also president of the Association of University Professors (1962-64). His writings have been translated into more than ten languages, and a listing of all of his scholarly publications and articles would number over 700. In economic theory he engaged in a famous controversy with the economist R.A. Lester over the meaning and significance of marginal analysis. He defended the importance of relative price changes in the description of international disturbances against the criticisms of Sidney Alexander. He has repeatedly emphasized the importance of precision when defining terms in economics, and a series of his essays in this vein was published under the title *Essays in Economic Semantics* (New York: New York University Press, 1975). He is best known for his work in international finance, which has absorbed his attention from his earliest book in German (1925) to a collection of his writings published under the title *International Payments, Debts, and Gold* (New York: Scribners, 1966). Machlup held the prestigious Walker chair in Economics and International Finance at Princeton University from 1960 to 1971 and is currently professor at New York University, New York City.

Laurence S. Moss was born on 13 November 1944 in New York City. He attended Queens College of the City University of New York, where he earned a B.A. (1965) and an M.A. (1967) in economics. He received both an M.A. and a Ph.D. in economics from Columbia University, New York (1971). His dissertation on Mountifort Longfield was nominated for the Ansley Award by the Department of Economics in 1971 and will be published in expanded form under the title *Mountifort Longfield: Ireland's First Professor of Political Economy* (Ottawa, Ill.; Green Hill Publishers, forthcoming). Moss attended Ludwig von Mises' New York seminars on a regular basis (1963-65). He has lectured at Fordham University,

Swarthmore College, and Columbia University's Seminar on Irish Studies. He is a frequent contributor to the journal *History of Political Economy* and is the author of a monograph entitled "Private Property Anarchism: An American Variant," in *Further Explorations in the Theory of Anarchism* (Blacksburg, Va.: University Publications, 1974). He is an assistant professor of economics at the University of Virginia, Charlottesville.

Murray N. Rothbard was born on 2 March 1926 in New York City. He attended Columbia University, where he earned both an M.A. and a Ph.D. in economics (1956). His dissertation was published under the title *The Panic of 1819* (New York: Columbia University Press, 1962). He attended Ludwig von Mises' New York seminars from 1949 to 1960. His comprehensive two-volume study on modern Austrian economic theory is entitled *Man, Economy, and State: A Treatise on Economic Principles* (New York: D. Van Nostrand, 1962). Rothbard has contributed to journals as diverse as the *American Economic Review* and the *Journal of the History of Ideas*. He has made significant contributions to economic theory, economic history, philosophy of science, and modern political science. He has been recognized by the *New York Times Magazine* and *Business Week* as one of the nation's foremost representatives of the libertarian position. His other scholarly works include: *America's Great Depression* (Kansas City: Sheed and Ward, 1975), *Power and Market* (Menlo Park, Calif.: Institute for Humane Studies, 1970), and *For a New Liberty* (New York: Macmillan Co., 1973). Rothbard is a professor of economics at the Polytechnic Institute of New York, New York City.

Karen Iversen Vaughn was born on 21 July 1944 in New York City. She attended Queens College of the City University of New York, where she earned a B.A. in economics (1966) and graduated cum laude with the Andrew Goodman Award for excellence in economics. She received an M.A. (1969) and a Ph.D. (1971) in economics from Duke University. Her dissertation was on "The Economic Theories of John Locke." Ms. Vaughn was named a fellow under the National Defense Education Act (1966-69) and pursued her research on Locke at the Bodleian Library at Oxford University in 1969. She has coauthored papers on economic theory published in the *Southern Economic Journal*. Her study "John Locke and the Morality of the Marketplace" will appear in *SPOUDAL*, a publication of the Piraeus Graduate School of Industrial Studies. Ms. Vaughn is an assistant professor of economics at the University of Tennessee, Knoxville.